Selections from Cicero *Philippic* II

The following titles are available from Bloomsbury

Selections from Apuleius *Metamorphoses* V: An Edition for Intermediate Students, with introduction, commentary notes and vocabulary by Stuart R. Thomson

Selections from Cicero *Philippic* II: An Edition for Intermediate Students, with introduction, commentary notes and vocabulary by Christopher Tanfield

Selections from Cicero *Pro Milone*: An Edition for Intermediate Students, with introduction by Lynn Fotheringham and commentary notes and vocabulary by Robert West

Selections from Horace *Odes:* An Edition for Intermediate Students, with introduction, commentary notes and vocabulary by John Godwin

Selections from Horace *Satires:* An Edition for Intermediate Students, with introduction, commentary notes and vocabulary by John Godwin

Selections from Ovid *Amores* II: An Edition for Intermediate Students, with introduction, commentary notes and vocabulary by Alfred Artley

Selections from Ovid *Heroides*: An Edition for Intermediate Students, with introduction, commentary notes and vocabulary by John Godwin

Selections from Propertius, Tibullus and Ovid: An Edition for Intermediate Students, with introduction, commentary notes and vocabulary by Anita Nikkanen

Selections from Tacitus *Annals* I: An Edition for Intermediate Students, with introduction by Roland Mayer and commentary notes and vocabulary by Katharine Radice

Selections from Tacitus *Histories* I: An Edition for Intermediate Students, with introduction by Ellen O'Gorman and commentary notes and vocabulary by Benedict Gravell

Selections from Virgil *Aeneid* VIII: An Edition for Intermediate Students, with introduction, commentary notes and vocabulary by Keith Maclennan

Selections from Virgil *Aeneid* X: An Edition for Intermediate Students, with introduction, commentary notes and vocabulary by Christopher Tanfield

Selections from Virgil *Aeneid* XI: An Edition for Intermediate Students, with introduction, commentary notes and vocabulary by Ashley Carter

Supplementary resources for these volumes can be found at
www.bloomsbury.com/bloomsbury-classical-languages
Please type the URL into your web browser and follow the instructions to access the Companion Website. If you experience any problems, please contact Bloomsbury at contact@bloomsbury.com

Selections from Cicero
Philippic II:
An Edition for Intermediate Students

Sections 44–50, 78–92, 100–119

With introduction, commentary notes and vocabulary by Christopher Tanfield

BLOOMSBURY ACADEMIC
Bloomsbury Publishing Inc
1385 Broadway, New York, NY 10018, USA
50 Bedford Square, London, WC1B 3DP, UK

BLOOMSBURY, BLOOMSBURY ACADEMIC and the Diana logo are
trademarks of Bloomsbury Publishing Plc

First published in Great Britain 2018 as *Cicero* Philippic *II: A Selection*
This edition first published in the United States of America 2019

Copyright © Christopher Tanfield, 2018, 2019

Cover image © Marco Lamberto / EyeEm

All rights reserved. No part of this publication may be reproduced or transmitted in any form or by any means, electronic or mechanical, including photocopying, recording, or any information storage or retrieval system, without prior permission in writing from the publishers.

Bloomsbury Publishing Inc does not have any control over, or responsibility for, any third-party websites referred to or in this book. All internet addresses given in this book were correct at the time of going to press. The author and publisher regret any inconvenience caused if addresses have changed or sites have ceased to exist, but can accept no responsibility for any such changes.

A catalog record for this book is available from the Library of Congress.

ISBN: PB: 978-1-5013-5030-6
ePDF: 978-1-5013-5032-0
eBook: 978-1-5013-5031-3

Series: Bloomsbury Classical Languages

Typeset by RefineCatch Limited, Bungay, Suffolk
Printed and bound in the United States of America

To find out more about our authors and books visit
www.bloomsbury.com and sign up for our newsletters.

Contents

Preface	vii
Introduction	1
Maps	29
Text	35
Commentary Notes	51
Vocabulary	137

Preface

The text and notes found in this volume are designed to guide any student who has mastered Latin at beginner's level and wishes to read a selection from Cicero's Second Philippic in the original.

The Second Philippic captures a dramatic moment when, in the year of Caesar's murder, Cicero seized the opportunity to attempt to rescue the senate and the apparatus of republican government from the power-mongers, above all Antony, who were now directing Roman politics. It was also the moment when the greatest orator of his time, one who had argued for so many defendants and causes, had to plead for himself. By now in his sixties, Cicero imparted to his rhetoric no less energy than in his earlier speeches, not least because the stakes were so high – but the same energy made this speech his own death-warrant, as well as securing it the lasting admiration of his contemporaries. It is still held to be one of his greatest achievements.

This edition contains a detailed introduction to the historical context of the Philippics, supported by two maps, and a brief guide to Cicero's oratory, with particular reference to this speech. The commentary which follows the text pays due attention therefore to the harder points of grammar and word order. It also explains the historical or cultural references which must be grasped along with the language. Further material may be found online at www.bloomsbury.com/bloomsbury-classical-languages a commentary on the stylistic features of the extracts, summaries of the passages before or between the extracts, a timeline for the year 44 BC and a chronology of Cicero's life. At the end of the book is a full vocabulary list for all the words contained in the chosen sections.

The text follows closely the Oxford Classical Text of A. C. Clark (1918), with one departure from its wording and very few from its punctuation. Of the greatest assistance has been the commentary of J. T. Ramsey. I am also immensely grateful to Robert West for his patient suggestions and amendments and Alice Wright and her team at Bloomsbury for all their support during the publication process. A great deal more remains to be said about the text which follows, but that must be left to the reader.

Christopher Tanfield
July 2017

Introduction

Historical Background

[All dates are BC.]

The events leading up to and following the Second Philippic

It is 44. Julius Caesar has been assassinated; his assassins have not taken control of government. Into the power vacuum spring first Antony (M. Antonius), Caesar's deputy, and soon afterwards Octavian, Julius Caesar's great nephew and main heir. They both have military support. Marcus Tullius Cicero, still the main orator of his day, wields his influence to a different end: he wants to safeguard the system of government which has developed over the centuries since the fall of the kings to prevent any one man from holding total sway – he is the champion of the Republic. He considers Antony its direst threat and so pens a series of speeches to attack him, the so-called 'Philippics'. These speeches incur Antony's bitter and personal antagonism; they are not merely attacks on Antony but also Cicero's all-or-nothing self-defence. Despite Cicero's roll call of success at the Roman bar, this time he loses – and a year later meets his death at the hands of Antony's executioners. At every turn in the second Philippic, the height of the risk he is running is audible in Cicero's intensity. It became regarded in antiquity as the work whose very quality ensured Cicero's own demise, and in our own day as a supreme example of both character assassination and magnificent defiance.

To understand its content, however, we must backtrack and add some historical detail. Julius Caesar, since 58 general of the Roman armies in Gaul, had added Gallia Comata (roughly speaking modern France and eastwards as far as the German border) to Roman territory. In 49, instead of relinquishing his command as the senate had instructed him to do, he led part of his army across the Rubicon, out of his area of jurisdiction and towards Rome. The senate, treating this as an act of war, placed its troops under the command of Gnaeus Pompeius Magnus (Pompey). Julius Caesar defeated Pompey at Pharsalus in 48; he then followed up his victory by centralising in himself more and more of the powers belonging to the most important offices of state, or to the senate itself. He then set about a programme of reforms designed to have popular appeal. The final straw came in 44, when he 'accepted' the appointment of 'dictator for life'. The position of dictator had always been reserved for emergencies and its tenure limited to six months; the only exception before Caesar had been Sulla, in 82, who had left such poisonous memories that Pompey, dealing with the crisis caused by Clodius's and Milo's gangs in 52, preferred to be called 'sole consul'. Caesar, by contrast, since reaching Rome in 49, had been named dictator first for six months (he relinquished the title after eleven days), then for one year, then for ten years, and at last in perpetuity. He had in effect made himself a king.

So a core of twenty senators along with some forty others, led by M. Iunius Brutus and C. Cassius Longinus, plotted Caesar's murder, to take place at a meeting of the Senate on the 15 (Ides) March 44. Of the conspirators known to us, nine or ten can be identified as Pompey's followers, subsequently pardoned by Caesar; another six, however, were Caesar's own adherents, who had fought for him in the civil war and become disillusioned after it. The plan nearly miscarried: Caesar, warned, some sources claim, by his wife Calpurnia not to attend and feeling unwell in any case, was about to send word to dismiss the assembled senators. One of the conspirators, however, D. Brutus, came to him and urged him to attend; another, C. Trebonius, detained M. Antonius (Antony), who was with Caesar, outside the Curia

Pompeia, which was the venue for the meeting. This enabled the attackers to fall upon their victim within; Caesar was stabbed, it is said, twenty-three times, and expired at the foot of Pompey's statue.

The senators not involved in the assassination, such as Cicero, fled the scene; the conspirators, who had expected an upsurge of approval but at a public gathering in the Forum found themselves unapplauded, took refuge on the Capitoline hill, protected by barricades and a force of gladiators. Cicero visited them there that same evening; they had opted to spare Caesar's deputies, Antony (consul for the year with Caesar) and the master of the horse, M. Lepidus, to convince the people that the assassination's aim was liberation from a single tyrant. Cicero, by contrast, advocated a clean sweep of Caesar's henchmen. The conspirators were not persuaded and Antony, who had holed up in his own house, took heart and gave orders to Lepidus, stationed just outside the city with a single legion, to occupy the Forum. Antony also visited Caesar's widow, Calpurnia, and from her acquired Caesar's papers. There followed a two-day stand-off, but, crucially, the Caesarian faction was now in command of the situation.

It was Antony who convened the senate on 17 March: in a deal mediated by Cicero, those who attended granted an amnesty to the 'Liberators' and ratified Caesar's *acta*, including bounties promised to veterans. This compromise averted further conflict and allowed the Liberators to descend from the Capitoline – on that evening, Brutus and Cassius dined with Antony and Lepidus. The compromise also gave Antony the opportunity to play on Caesar's popularity beyond the grave: two days later, when Caesar's will was opened soon after the session of the senate, it nominated his great nephew Gaius Octavius (henceforth in these notes referred to by his new cognomen, 'Octavian') as his principal heir. It also announced that Caesar had left generous legacies to the Roman people and made a minor heir of one of his murderers. A few days later Antony was able to exploit the brewing sense of an injustice done when, at Caesar's funeral, by his oration he so inflamed his listeners' loyalties that they took the body, destined for cremation outside the boundaries of the city, and burned it on an improvised pyre in the Forum itself. The crowd then attempted to set fire to the houses of Caesar's killers; Brutus, Cassius and their associates promptly retreated for a short while from Rome for their own safety. Left in possession of the field, Antony nevertheless stopped short of creating mayhem and instead carried through two measures which conciliated his opponents, not least Cicero – abolishing the office of dictator and limiting the implementation of several of Caesar's projects not yet begun. And when a demagogue known as pseudo-Marius returned from exile and tried to ride the wave of pro-Caesarian sentiment by stirring up anger against Caesar's assassins – he erected (in mid-April) an altar on the site of Caesar's cremation in the Forum – Antony, no doubt jealous of his own supremacy, did not hesitate to have pseudo-Marius annihilated.

By then Cicero had left Rome for his Italian estates; he busied himself with philosophical writings and then, in July, set off for Greece to visit his son Marcus in Athens. He did not envisage returning to Rome until Antony surrendered his consulship at the end of the year, but in the event became storm-bound on the Sicilian straits near Rhegium from where, in August, he made his decision to return to Rome. He was not alone in abandoning the capital: some of the Liberators with provinces (such as D. Brutus) had already made their way to their various destinations; M. Brutus and C. Cassius, the praetors, felt sufficiently uncomfortable at Rome to follow Cicero's example, about 12 April.

In the meantime, Antony was consolidating his position in Rome: as Cicero's letters have it, even before Cicero left the city on 7 April, Antony had started embezzling the resources Caesar had stored in the Temple of Ops for his Parthian campaign. Antony was also issuing in Caesar's name laws and decrees of his own concoction (at any rate according to Cicero), which under the terms of the senate's accord (*senatus consultum*) of 17 March had to be respected. Nevertheless, during April, Antony and Cicero corresponded with each other, Antony consulting Cicero and Cicero answering affably. By now, in any case, Antony faced another problem: on 18 April, Octavian had reached Naples, where many of Caesar's previous veterans had been settled; he had adopted the name C. Iulius Caesar, as he was allowed to do under the terms of Caesar's will, and despite his youth (he was only 18) was gathering a considerable body of support among them. Antony therefore took advantage of the senate's spring recess to visit the settlements, shore up his own support, and identify land for distribution to Caesar's latest body of veterans due for retirement. Octavian in reaction proceeded to Rome in early May, accepted Caesar's inheritance and announced his intention both to pay out Caesar's legacies to the people and to hold public games in Caesar's honour. Also during Antony's absence from Rome – but before Octavian's arrival there – P. Dolabella, who had been appointed consul to replace Caesar, had taken down a monument to Caesar in the Forum and severely punished those who were trying to give Caesar divine status. This had raised Cicero's hopes that M. Brutus and C. Cassius, the praetors, and others of the Liberators, might have been safe to reappear in Rome; but Antony put paid to this idea when he returned from his Campanian tour with an intimidating bodyguard of Caesar's veterans. Having such a force behind him, Antony was able both to woo Dolabella, promising him extended office, and to refuse to release to Octavian the funds Octavian needed to pay for Caesar's legacies and the games Octavian had promised in Caesar's honour. In the end, Octavian met these immense expenses through the generosity of rich friends of Caesar's.

The drawback to Antony of his gang, however, was that, when the senate met again on 1 June, many of the senators stayed away. Undeterred, Antony took his proposals directly to the Assembly, which, on 3 June, passed a plebiscite giving him and Dolabella five-year governorships of provinces (instead of two-year) after their consulships were over. Antony quickly exchanged his allocated province of Macedonia for Gaul, but kept for himself five of the six legions massed in Macedonia in preparation for the campaign which Caesar had projected against the Parthians. The swap of provinces also entitled him to take over the three legions in Cisalpine Gaul under the command of D. Brutus, another of the Liberators, possibly before D. Brutus's term of office was completed. These legions constituted the only standing army in Italy and were vital for the anti-Caesarians as a counterweight to Antony's military presence in Rome. It looked as though Antony was going to follow closely in his former commander Caesar's footsteps, crossing the Rubicon to topple the senatorial government.

Antony further bolstered his position by causing the senate, at their meeting on 5 June, to assign to the still absent praetors M. Brutus and C. Cassius an overseas grain commission – thereby insulting and sidelining them simultaneously. On the other hand, later in the same month, under a *lex agraria* he set up a Board of Seven magistrates (*VIIviri*) to redistribute land in Italy; the Board's chairman was L. Antonius, Antony's brother, and its members were Antony, Dolabella and other confederates of Antony. The popular influence of the Board was enormous. M. Brutus and C. Cassius countered from outside Rome by lobbying for the repeal of their appointment to the overseas grain commission. M. Brutus moreover made lavish plans for the *ludi Apollinares* in the first half of July, which he as city praetor was tasked with organising, and only reluctantly stayed away for the event itself, delegating a colleague to preside over it. The favourable reception of the games, combined with now open hostility between Antony and Octavian, encouraged Brutus and Cassius to hope that Antony would be forced to make concessions to them, but at the meeting of the senate called for 1 August, despite the Liberators exhorting their supporters to let themselves be heard, the only anti-Caesarian voice in the chamber was that of L. Calpurnius Piso, who soon realised his isolation and did not attend the senate the following day.

For the impetus had already shifted away from the Liberators since the *ludi Apollinares* finished in mid-July: in late July, Octavian staged his games in honour of Caesar – and, as luck would have it, a comet appeared in the sky, visible during the day, which was interpreted as the ascent of Caesar among the gods. It is probable that Octavian began his distribution of Caesar's legacies at the same period. But, just as the rift between him and Antony seemed to be widening, Caesar's veterans intervened and compelled Antony and Octavian to meet on the Capitoline hill and renounce their enmity. Thus Antony, instead of feeling on the back foot on 1 August, felt confident enough to issue a threatening and insulting edict against M. Brutus and C. Cassius. They responded with a defiant letter and an edict of their own, then set sail with the small flotillas they had assembled for their overseas grain commissions to assemble an army in the eastern provinces.

On 17 August, M. Brutus on his way to Greece reached Velia, on the south-western coast of Italy. There he found Cicero, who had, while at Rhegium, received a report from Rome that some form of rapprochement was feasible between Antony and the Liberators. This, combined with criticism of his decision to leave the city as an act of desertion, had made him resolve to go back. Brutus's account of the reconciliation between Antony and Octavian did not put Cicero off. He reached his villa at Pompeii on 19 August and Rome itself on 1 September. Antony was expecting him – he had, the day before, called a meeting of the senate in the Temple of Concord, seeking approval for his proposal that an extra day be added in Caesar's honour to all public thanksgivings. This was anathema to Cicero, who in any case felt it legitimate, since he had only just returned, not to attend: he sent his excuses on grounds of fatigue. Antony threatened to send public slaves round to smash the doors of Cicero's house. The following day, when the senate met again in the Temple of Concord, Cicero delivered his so-called *First Philippic*. He began it by explaining his departure from Rome in April and his absence from the session the previous day, slipping in several references to his friendly ties to Antony. Nonetheless, he specified that, if he had been present, he would have voted against the additional honour to Caesar. The second, longer, part of the speech had two avowed aims: firstly to persuade the senate to reassert its authority in the face of Antony's intimidation and, secondly, to argue for a change of behaviour from Antony himself. Turning to this second aim, Cicero portrayed Antony's most recent policies as betrayals of Caesar's own legislation (an attempt by Cicero to alienate Antony's Caesarian loyalists); he also laced his descriptions of Antony's activities with innuendo of corruption, forgery, bribery and bullying – themes to which he would overtly return in the *Second Philippic*.

Antony took immediate umbrage, summoned a meeting of the senate for 19 September (the earliest possible date given the intervening *ludi Romani* and *dies comitiales*, for on these the Assembly could be called together but not the senate) and took himself off to a villa at Tibur with a teacher of rhetoric, Sextus Clodius, to work on his riposte. When 19 September came, the tabled business was the decree of a *supplicatio*, or public thanksgiving, to L. Plancus, consul designate for 42, in recognition of his victories in Gallia Comata. The Temple of Concord was surrounded by Antony's armed men; its doors were, contrary to custom, closed; and members of Antony's bodyguard were even insinuated into the main body of the temple. After the official business, Antony delivered his scathing assault on Cicero. But Cicero was not there: although it seems he would have been expected to attend for a vote on a *supplicatio* and he himself had wished, as he wrote to Plancus afterwards, to express his support for it, it was simply too dangerous for him to attend. He later claimed his own inclination to go had been overruled by his friends' concern for his welfare.

So Cicero, leaving Rome for his country villas, set to work on the *de Amicitia*, the *de Officiis* and the retort to Antony which is the *Second Philippic*. He submitted a first draft to his close friend and confidant

Atticus on 25 October (*ad Att.* 15.13a), saying that Atticus could publish it at his own discretion though he himself could not foresee when the appropriate time would come – for now, Cicero favoured dignified silence; he remarked that this speech of his would never see the light of day until the Republic was restored. A letter to Atticus of 5 November approves several suggested amendments (*ad Att.* 16.11). He himself had no intention of attending the senate until Antony had stepped down and the new consuls, Hirtius and Pansa, assumed office in the new year. Nevertheless, on 20 December, spurred on by Antony's evacuation of the city and the arrival of an edict from D. Brutus in Cisalpine Gaul declaring his refusal to hand over his province to Antony, Cicero did appear – and delivered the *Third Philippic*, which advocated solidarity with D. Brutus and Octavian. That same day, in the afternoon, Cicero delivered the *Fourth Philippic* to the Assembly, in which he pronounced Antony a public enemy and affirmed that peace with him was inconceivable. This moment, or shortly before, was probably the time when he circulated our *Second Philippic*. Whatever the timing, henceforth Antony's enmity towards Cicero was implacable.

The speech is cast as if it had been delivered in the acrimonious atmosphere of 19 September – to an audience including Antony himself. The pretence is sustained by references to the circumstances of that day as well as by frequent addresses to Antony and comments to the senators on how Antony is alarmed, ashamed, angered by what Cicero is saying. It scrupulously avoids mentioning events which happened after that date, however much they would have enhanced Cicero's case. Cicero wishes to demonstrate what he would have said at that meeting of the senate; and while that might seem a poor second to actually delivering the speech, it clearly reached an avid readership, whether friend or foe, and being the longest of all the Philippics and the most extreme in its vitriol had the most damning effect – on Cicero as well as on Antony.

While Cicero was engaged on his composition of the *Second Philippic*, Antony was preoccupied with manoeuvres against Octavian: going, on 9 October, to Brundisium to take command of the legions arriving from Macedonia, he made allegations to them (which Cicero and others were inclined to believe) that Octavian had been implicated in an assassination attempt on him. Octavian's agents meanwhile stirred up disaffection among these very troops; Octavian himself, exploiting Antony's absence from Rome and playing upon his adopted name of C. Iulius Caesar, recruited an army from Caesar's veterans of his own and, entering the city on 9 November, gave a powerful address to the people. Antony made haste back to the capital with his freshly-acquired legions – only to find two of them desert him for Octavian, who had prudently retired to the north of the city. It was Antony's turn to take to his heels, on 28/29 November, in the direction of Cisalpine Gaul, where he had soldiers still faithful to him and where he planned to relieve D. Brutus of his provincial command with its associated forces. Cicero, who had been back in Rome since 9 December and was in correspondence with D. Brutus, felt secure in attending the senate on 20 December, when, as already mentioned, D. Brutus's edict was recited refusing to surrender his province to Antony, and Cicero delivered his rallying cry in favour of D. Brutus and Octavian against Antony.

When the consuls for 43, A. Hirtius and C. Vibius Pansa, took office, Antony was besieging D. Brutus in Mutina. Cicero spent the next months locked in opposition to the numerous peace-mongers in the senate, delivering the series of speeches which are also grouped within the Philippics (the *Fifth* onwards); it took till 15 April for the senate's army, under the consuls, to engage Antony at Mutina. Though it was a victory for the republicans, Pansa died of wounds. On 21 April, Cicero delivered his *Fourteenth Philippic*, reminding his hearers that Antony was yet to be declared a public enemy and Mutina yet to be relieved. Almost as he was speaking, however, a second battle was taking place, another republican victory, though in it Hirtius was killed.

Without consuls, the republican cause lost momentum; D. Brutus's troops deserted to Octavian, Antony in retreat secured the allegiance of commanders in Spain and the rest of Gaul, including Lepidus. Octavian marched on Rome with his army to obtain one of the vacant consulships then, having set out ostensibly to take on Antony, on 27 November 43, signed a pact with him, brokered by Lepidus – the so-called 'Second Triumvirate'. Part of settling their differences was settling old scores; Cicero was proscribed, hunted down and murdered. On Antony's instructions, his head and hands were cut off and displayed on the Rostra in the Forum, as his recompense for leading the war party and composing the Philippics.

The uncompromising and provocative style of these speeches, delivered (or, in the case of the *Second Philippic*, circulated) at a time when Cicero was shaping policy to a degree unknown since he suppressed the Catilinarian conspiracy, ensured that they were swiftly copied and disseminated. Thus C. Cassius, on the south coast of Italy, had read the *First Philippic*, delivered on 2 September, before the month was out. This importance, combined with their quality (Plutarch, *Life of Cicero* 24.6, says they were the speeches to which Cicero devoted most labour) gave them high prestige in antiquity. Juvenal (*Satire* X, 125 – see online commentary, §118) speaks of *conspicuae divina Philippica famae* ('divine Philippic of illustrious reputation'); Tacitus (*Dialogus de Oratoribus*, 37) argues that the dignity of the subject is what inspires great oratory, citing Catiline, Milo, Verres and – not just last in chronology – Antony. Already before the mid-first century AD, it had become a rhetorical exercise in the schools for students to put the case that, on condition of immunity from Antony, Cicero should burn his Philippics (Seneca, *Suasoriae* 7; Quintilian, *Institutio Oratoria* 3.8.46). The valedictory tone which Cicero strikes at the end of this *Second Philippic* reflects all too starkly that he had no such option.

The sources relevant to the Philippics

Mud sticks, and Cicero's Philippics have been epitomised as 'an eternal monument of eloquence, of rancour and of misrepresentation' (Ronald Syme, quoted by Ramsey). Detaching oneself from the spectacle of Antony besmirched is not always easy, especially because Cicero's own account in the Philippics was often swallowed by later historians and rival versions of events have largely been lost.

Some 200 of Cicero's letters, which include correspondence from D. and M. Brutus and Antony, belong to the period April 44 to July 43 – and, because they were never intended for publication, allow real insights into the views and feelings of the writers. Cicero's own opinions sometimes prefigure in thought or language what appears in the Philippics themselves, but can also be at variance. The reader of these letters is still in Cicero's orbit, but not in the stranglehold of a speech.

Of contemporary historians, only fragments and summaries of Livy survive for the period between the Civil War and the death of Cicero (*Ab Urbe Condita* books 109–120) – though one of the fragments is precisely his description of the death of Cicero. Asinius Pollio, praetor in 45 and consul in 40, wrote a history covering the years from 60 to the Battle of Philippi in 42, in many of whose major events he had participated – such as the Battle of Pharsalus in 48. All that can be reassembled of his narrative are traces preserved by the later historians Appian (*fl.* AD 130) and Dio Cassius (*fl.* AD 200), who also retain detectable elements of Livy. Asinius Pollio is less kind than Livy in his narration of Cicero's final hours. One fragment from Augustus's memoirs, where he mentions the daylight comet in July, has been caught in the amber of Pliny's Natural History. The diplomat Nicolaus of Damascus, writing in Greek at the end of the first century BC, in what remains of his biography of Augustus, gives what is probably an eyewitness account of the events of the Ides of March.

The early imperial historians Valerius Maximus and Velleius Paterculus, writing under Tiberius in the first century AD, have preserved anecdotal evidence and, in the former case, some strands of Livy. Though later, Suetonius (*fl.* AD 100) has conserved more of service in his *Life of Caesar* and *Life of Augustus*, as has Plutarch (*fl.* AD 90) in his lives of Caesar, Cicero, Pompey, Brutus and Antony – even if the last, owing to its clear acceptance of much of the material in the *Second Philippic*, cannot be treated as independent historical confirmation.

Of later historians, Appian and Dio Cassius have already been mentioned. Dio Cassius, like Plutarch, cannot resist the gravitational pull of the *Second Philippic*, even down to his attribution of motives. Nevertheless, he, like Appian, furnishes additional material. Subsequent authors, from the second to the fifth centuries – Florus, Eutropius, Orosius and Julius Obsequens – occasionally salvage shards of Livy. None of them is cited in this commentary.

Oratory

Types of speech and structure

Rhetorical textbooks started with the Greeks – from his first work on rhetoric onwards, Cicero makes liberal reference to them and above all to Aristotle ('who of all men has supplied the greatest number of aids and ornaments to this art', *de Inventione* 1.5). Aristotle's division of speeches into three types (*Rhetoric* 1.3) – συμβουλευτικόν, δικανικόν, and ἐπιδεικτικόν – became the Roman genera *deliberativum*, *iudicale* and *demonstrativum*, as anatomised in the early (late 80s BC) treatise *Rhetorica ad Herennium* (1.2). Of these genera:

- *deliberativum* argues for and against policy;
- *iudicale* presents a legal case or addresses a legal controversy;
- *demonstrativum* praises or attacks an individual.

The *Second Philippic* belongs to the third genus. To each genus of speech a particular structure was appropriate. The general components of any speech are defined by the *Rhetorica ad Herennium* (1.4) following Aristotle (*Rhetoric* 3.13) and, in large measure, common sense, as:

- *Exordium* (introduction)
- *Narratio* (statement of facts)
- *Divisio* (table of contents)
- *Confirmatio* (argument for one's own case)
- *Confutatio* (argument against what the adversary has said)
- *Conclusio* (peroration, the grand finale).

Turning to the *genus demonstrativum* in particular, the *Rhetorica* (3.10–15) suggests that there might be no need for the *narratio*, that the *divisio* contain the programme of what is to be praised and what blamed and that the detail of the praise and blame follow (as *confirmatio* and *confutatio*). This analysis (following Ramsey, though keeping to the section names of the *Rhetorica*) is what has been used in the commentary. Because replying to Antony, the *confutatio* precedes the *confirmatio*. The progression from the first to the second is signalled by a so-called *transitio*, a minor component to orientate the hearer (*Rhetorica* 4.35). Cicero could treat his components with a degree of flexibility – thus the *divisio* comes after Cicero has already loosed off some preliminary salvos against Antony.

The *Rhetorica*, in discussing the *genus demonstrativum* (3.13–14), helpfully lists headings under which to generate praise or blame:

- external circumstances – birth, education
- physical appearance – attractive features, abilities, (failure in) compensating for the lack of them
- character – behaviour when in power, use of wealth, treatment of friends, bravery, temperance etc.

Such checklists guaranteed that any eulogy, or character assassination, would be truly comprehensive. Cicero's examination of Antony certainly aims at comprehensiveness, and though it is anything but standard, he might well have employed such an aide-memoire when compiling his material.

Rhetorical style

The *Rhetorica ad Herennium*, as well as structure, defines (1.3) the ingredients of the speech as follows – the explanations in brackets are taken from Cicero's *de Oratore*, 1.142:

- *inventio* (finding out what to say)
- *dispositio* (disposing and arranging the material, not only in a certain order, but with a degree of power and judgment)
- *elocutio* (clothing thoughts with language)
- *memoria* (securing them in the memory)
- *pronuntiatio* (delivering them with dignity and grace).

Inventio and *dispositio* have been examined (however briefly) in paragraph 1 above. The second, *dispositio*, however, also governs the next ingredient, *elocutio* (see, for example, Quintilian *Institutio Oratoria* 8 pr. 6). This use of language to create large-scale structure tends to escape comment, not least from the ancient treatises themselves – so the best way to see such detailed architecture is to look at an illustration:

> In paragraphs 80 to 84, Cicero relates the episode of Antony's using his office as augur to block Dolabella's appointment as consul. Cicero's contention is that Antony, as consul, could have blocked Dolabella's appointment more effectively than he did as an augur – and that the course he chose was unbelievably stupid. First Cicero introduces Antony sarcastically as *hic bonus augur* (§80). Then (§81) he makes his point, 'Couldn't you have done this better through your consular rather

than your priestly rank?' – *si augur non esses et consul esses*. Cicero then goes on to differentiate what the two roles can do, concluding that Antony is ignorant of this – *nec scit quod augurem ... decet*. Next, in §82, he parodies Antony's curious meekness as **consul**; he resumes, in §83, Antony's behaviour as **augur** – 'With this done, our good augur ...' (*confecto negotio, bonus augur ...*), echoing §80. He repeats his description of Antony's misdemeanours and makes a climax (§83) of the deliberate absurdity, 'As an augur you impeded an augur, as a consul a consul' (*augur auguri, consul consuli obnuntiasti*) – harping on Antony's double powers. Cicero's two final questions (§84) are first whether Antony, acting as augur, was even sober – recapitulating all the references to ignorance or incompetence in these chapters (*incredibilem stupiditatem; imperite; homine numquam sobrio; inscientia; nec scit ...*); and recapitulating Antony's disrespect (*impudentia* x 3; *adrogantiam ... insolentiamque*). His second question, what force his utterance might have had, Cicero asks as an augur himself – and by implication a *bonus augur*: So the episode is rounded off. On the page, this can seem heavy-handed or repetitious but, when spoken with due drama, drums home what might otherwise seem an insistence on abstruse protocol. In *de Oratore* 292, Cicero has his spokesman Antonius remark: 'In pleading, my usual method is to fix on whatever strong points a cause has and to illustrate and make the most of them, dwelling on them, insisting on them, clinging to them'.

Within *elocutio* fall both the structure of individual sentences (syntax) and the familiar devices such as alliteration, anaphora, chiasmus and so on. Regarding syntax, the *Second Philippic* is punchier than some of Cicero's more periodic and casuistic speeches – it does not seek to obfuscate by piling clauses on one another, or by nesting clauses within one another, but to hit home as hard as possible. This requires clarity – even in innuendo. There are frequent rhetorical questions and exclamations, allowing the pace of the speech to slow down and pick up again. Ramsey comments:

Ornamentation tends to play a subordinate role to vigour in expressing the message, and the speaker keeps his eye on the goal, which is always to persuade. He reserves elaborate sentences for those occasions where he wishes to lend variety or avoid monotony, and periodic sentences tend to be of the type where the leading idea is stated early, with elaboration coming afterwards.

(Introduction 3, 'Aim and Style')

Add to this that such elaboration is often paratactic (i.e. clauses in parallel with or without conjunctions and without subordination – which is easier to assimilate).

Of rhetorical devices, or 'figures of speech', the fourth book of the *Rhetorica ad Herennium* gives a compendium; the ones mentioned in the commentary are glossed in '4. Rhetorical Terms' below. Those interested in the exhaustive (and exhausting) richness of rhetorical terminology might profitably consult 'Silva Rhetoricae' (http://rhetoric.byu.edu/). It is vital, however, always to treat these devices as achieving a particular effect in a particular context, not as ends in themselves. Thus alliteration in one place will not be trying to achieve the same thing as alliteration in another; the use of 'alliteration' as a term in isolation is all but meaningless and the further explanation you give might even make it unnecessary: e.g. 'The recurrent 't' expresses Cicero's irritation ...'

The importance of *memoria* is self-evident, as Cicero observes (*de Oratore* 2.355), given the length and complexity of a speech and the impossibility of simply reciting from notes. The techniques for training memory (e.g. *de Oratore* 3.356 ff.) are not relevant here, but are worth an experiment.

Pronuntiatio likewise lies outside the scope of this introduction. As the drawing together of all the ingredients, however, it seems to become paramount in Cicero's own thinking on oratory. In his early work *de Inventione*, he showed an appetite similar to that of the *Rhetorica ad Herennium* for anatomising the components of a speech;

in his later work *de Oratore* (55 BC, 1.5) he had grown dissatisfied with this approach by recipe – 'What came from my notebooks when I was a youth hardly seems appropriate to my age and experience now'. Thus, in *de Oratore*, he is more concerned with the broader education of the orator and, though he does not ignore structure, is less interested in its nuts and bolts and more with how to deliver an affecting performance (2.188: 'It is not possible that the judge should feel concern, or hate, or envy, or fear in any degree, or that he should be moved to compassion and tears, unless all those sensations which the orator would awaken in the judge shall appear to be deeply felt and experienced by the orator himself.'). By the time Cicero was composing the Philippics, to judge from *Orator* (46 BC), his focus had moved on again. Defending his own 'Roman' style against those who espoused Athenian models, he emphasises his Latinity – in particular the sound (*sonus*) and rhythm (*numerus*) of the language and the way these could delight the ears of his listeners (163). He goes to extraordinary lengths in describing rhythm (174–229). Its use to provide a resounding end to a long period, or to break up a long period into its natural sense components (*cola*), through recognisable metrical units known as *clausulae* (see 'Clausulae' below) is not the whole of it – attention to rhythm permeates the whole sentence (199). He says he has seen meetings burst into spontaneous applause at a felicitous cadence (168). The orator, in Cicero's depiction, becomes a virtuoso composer/performer in an almost musical sense, modulating pace, tone of voice and gesture in keeping with what he says. It is therefore all the more important – indeed it is perhaps the only way to appreciate the text – once aware of its properties, to read it out loud.

Cicero and Demosthenes

The name 'Philippics' was given to this series of speeches by Cicero himself, jokingly (*iocans*) when referring to two of the series which he had sent with a letter to Brutus (now missing), which Brutus acknowledged on 1 April 43 (*ad Brutum* 2.3.4). Cicero replied (*ad Brutum* 2.4.2) with the promise to send him more, '... since I see that you like my 'Philippics''. Thereafter the name stuck, as Plutarch remarks (*Life of Cicero* 48.6) – 'Cicero himself entitled his speeches against Antony 'Philippics', and to this day the documents are called Philippics'.

The reference is to the Athenian orator Demosthenes, who, between 351 and 341, had delivered four speeches urging his fellow-citizens to take action against Philip of Macedon. The latter's military expansion was threatening to (and eventually did) absorb Athens, much as Antony's was threatening to (and did, with Octavian's) destroy the Republic. Even in 60 Cicero had sent his friend Atticus some political speeches mentioning how Demosthenes had in his Philippics made the transition from forensic to political oratory (*ad Att.* 2.1.3); but it was particularly towards the end of his life that Cicero's admiration for his Greek predecessor became more explicit. Three late works on rhetoric (*Brutus*, *Orator* and *de Optimo Genere Oratorum*) give Demosthenes pride of place as the exemplar. Thus Cicero writes in *Orator* (132, 133):

> 'But ... it is not any particular force of genius, but an exceeding energy of disposition which inflames me to such a degree that I cannot restrain myself; nor would anyone who listens to a speech ever be inflamed, if the speech which reached his ears was not itself a fiery one (*ardens*)... If we are still on the look-out for examples, we must take them from Demosthenes, and we must cite them from that passage in the speech on the trial of Ctesiphon, where he ventures to speak of his own actions and counsels and services to the republic. That oration in truth corresponds so much to that idea which is implanted in our minds that no higher eloquence need be looked for.'

The speech to which Cicero is referring is not, in fact, one of the *Philippics* but Demosthenes's *de Corona*, which like Cicero's *Second Philippic* is both a personal defence and a demolition of his opponent, Aeschines, by going through his deeds from youth. Cicero says (*de Optimo Genere Oratorum* 14) that he has translated both this speech and the speech by Aeschines to which it was a reply; even if this was something he intended to do but never did, the intention itself is significant. Here is a flavour (*de Corona* 272–3) of the part Cicero especially admired:

> 'For if, when I took part in the discussion of public affairs, I had had absolute power, it would have been possible for all of you, the other orators, to lay the blame on me. But if you were present at every meeting of the Assembly; if the city always brought forward questions of policy for public consideration; if at the time my policy appeared the best to everyone, and above all to you (for it was certainly from no goodwill that you relinquished to me the hopes, the admiration, the honours, which all attached themselves to my policy at that time, but obviously because the truth was too strong for you, and you had nothing better to propose); then surely you are guilty of monstrous iniquity, in finding fault today with a policy than which, at the time, you could propose nothing better.'
>
> (Trans.: A.W. Pickard-Cambridge)

Rhetorical terms

adnominatio/paronomasia A pun, intended to make a particular thought surprising and/or memorable: e.g. *nec . . . est . . . postulanda* **prudentia**, *sed videte* **impudentiam**. [§81]

alliteration, consonance Strictly, repeated initial consonants, but used more loosely. See also **assonance, consonance** below. The effect is heavily dependent on the context: e.g. scorn in *quae potest esse turpitudinis tantae defensio?* [§85]

anacoluthon A break-down in strict syntax. This suggests thinking out loud, or becoming so carried away by content that form takes second place: e.g. the way the relative clause tails off after *tamen* in *qui cum de vectigalibus eximebatur . . . tamen infligi magnum rei publicae vulnus putabamus* [§101, where see note]

anadiplosis Picking up the word/idea at the end of one clause or sentence and starting the next with it. This either advances a chain of reasoning to the next step or simply emphasises that word/idea: e.g. . . . *ignores? nescis* . . . [§101]

anaphora Repetition of a word at the start of successive phrases or clauses – exerting a strong grip on the audience: e.g. **haec** *te* . . . *lacerat,* **haec** *te cruentat oratio* [§86]

anastrophe Strictly the inversion of word order between two words to give the unusually placed word special prominence: e.g. *invectus est copiosius* **multo** . . . [§79]

anthypophora Posing a question and then answering it yourself. §86 is built on this principle.

antiphrasis The use of a word so ironically as to mean its opposite: e.g. *nihil queror* [§79]

antithesis Contrast of two ideas so that the effect of each is enhanced by the other: e.g. **nihil** *ipse poterat;* **omnia** *rogabat* [§82]

apostrophe Turning from one audience to address another – present, absent or even non-existent: e.g. Cicero, after talking directly to Antony, appeals to the senators themselves: e.g. *Non dissimulat, patres conscripti* [§84]

assonance, consonance Strictly the repetition of a vowel sound (assonance) or a mid-word consonant (consonance) in the stressed syllables of neighbouring words. Assonance can be used for the repetition of whole syllables, or for initial vowels. See also **alliteration**. More loosely used when the repetition is outside the stressed syllables. The effect varies from onomatopoeia to emotional reinforcement: e.g. *quae quidem Caesar eg***isse***t, non ea quae eg***isse** *Caesarem dix***isse***t Antonius* [§101]

asyndeton Absence of conjunctions between words, clauses or whole sentences. The effect is one of sparseness or a faster pace. It can enhance an **antithesis**: e.g. **Medico** *tria milia iugerum: quid, si te sanasset?* **rhetori** *duo: quid, si te disertum facere potuisset?* [§101]

captatio benevolentiae Ensuring the goodwill of the speaker's hearers by appropriate compliments – Cicero (*de Oratore* 2.115) features it among the three prerequisites of persuasion: e.g. Cicero flatters his audience that they know what he is going to say better than he does [§47]

chiasmus a-b-b-a formation of ideas (or grammatical forms). It can either contrast the central two components by juxtaposition, or emphasise the outer ones, or both: e.g. *postea sum cultus a te, tu a me observatus* [§49], where the outer components (*cultus ... observatus*) enclose *a te ... a me* – the *tu* in the very centre is not part of the chiasmus but acts as a hinge.

concessio Granting something as if minor to move on to something more important: e.g. *esto: hoc imperite* [§81] where Cicero pretends to make allowances for something which is at best embarrassing.

conduplicatio Exact repetition of words or phrases, often qualified the second time – for leaden emphasis: e.g. *hunc unum diem, unum ... hodiernum diem* [§112]

correctio/epanorthosis Self-correction, to add the fruit of deeper and therefore more convincing thought: e.g. *... si hoc est explere, expilare quod statim effundas* [§50]. If this reading is correct, it is also an instance of **paronomasia**.

dilemma Offering an opponent the choice between two equally undesirable alternatives (and nothing else): e.g. *si nihil est ... sin est aliqua vis ...* [§84], where Cicero suggests either Antony was either drunk or incompetent.

doublet See **pleonasm**.

ellipse Omission of a word or phrase easily understood from the context – for compression and speed: e.g. *gemitus toto foro. unde diadema?* [§85]

epistrophe Repetition of a word at the end of successive clauses or sentences (cf. **anaphora**), for a strong link between the ideas: e.g.

*ad haec quae ... in maximis rei publicae miseriis **fecit**, et ad ea quae cotidie **facit** ...* [§47]

exclamatio/ecphonesis Outburst to communicate the speaker's own emotional commitment – very frequent in this speech: e.g. *quotiens te pater eius domu sua eiecit ...!* [§45]

figura etymologica The use of two words with the same etymological derivation in close proximity to one another, for comic effect or emphasis: e.g. *facinora effecit* [§109]

geminatio Doubling up a word so as to dwell on it: e.g. *iam iam minime miror ...* [§87]

hendiadys Using two nouns instead of one noun and a qualifier – makes for stronger impact: e.g. *vi manuque* [§91]

homoioteleuton (homoioptoton) Using the same ending in adjacent words or phrases – can have an effect from jingling to hammering: e.g. *studi**orum** enim su**orum** receptac**ulum** M. Varro voluit illud, non libid**inum** deversor**ium*** [§104]

hyperbaton Word order disrupted for effect – sometimes subtle, sometimes violent: e.g. *sed **nullum** est istuc ... praesidium* [§112]

hyperbole Rhetorical exaggeration; functions as in English, though Roman authors had more of a taste for it than contemporary ones have: e.g. *natabant pavimenta vino* [§105]

isocolon A series of sense units (clause or shorter) having the same grammatical structure; syntactical parallelism – the effect varies from soothing to relentless: e.g. *quid videras, quid senseras, quid audieras?* [§83]

litotes Understatement through a double negative (cf 'not infrequently' in English) – also used ironically as an intensative (so that 'not infrequently' substitutes for 'all the time'): e.g. *minime avara* [§113]

metaphor As in English – illustrating one context by words appropriate to another: e.g. *... libidinosi, avari, facinerosi verae laudis **gustatum** non habent* [§115]

metonymy Where something is referred to by one of its attributes (cf. **synecdoche**) – the effect is picturesque: e.g. *si ab hasta, valeat hasta* [§103], where *hasta* is the sign of an auction sale.

paronomasia Punning word-play – see **adnominatio** above.

pleonasm – doublet Repeating an idea in more than one word (Cicero favours doublets); to linger on the meaning: e.g. *grandiferae et fructuosae* [§101]

polyptoton Using the same word with different inflections more than once in close proximity. The effect can be simply to stress an idea, but can, particularly when combined with other devices such as **anaphora**, border on the obsessive: e.g. *decoxisse . . . decoctoribus . . . decoxisset* [§44]

polysyndeton Using conjunctions between every member (word, phrase, clause) of a list, to pile one thing on another: e.g. *at iste . . .* ***neque*** *. . .* ***et*** *. . . statim****que*** *. . .* [§109]

praeteritio / paralipsis Attracting attention to something by ostentiously passing over it: e.g. *sed iam stupra et flagitia omittamus* [§47]

prosopopoeia Personification, endowing abstract objects with human sensibilities: e.g. *o tecta ipsa misera . . .* [§104]

prothesis Addition of a syllable at the start of a word – either for poetic effect or to enable a contrast: e.g. *nunc ut similis tui, sed certe ut* ***dis****similis esset sui* [§107]

rhetorical question Asking a question without expecting an answer, either because none could be given, because the answer is obvious or because the speaker offers an answer of his own (see **anthypophora**). This particular device is ubiquitous in our extracts: e.g. *visne igitur te inspiciamus a puero?* [§44]

syllepsis Where one word governs or modifies two or more others in different ways – can be used humorously, or to give a (diverting) pause for thought: e.g. *sed ad iter Italiamque redeamus* [§101], which probably means 'let us revert to the (topic of) your journey and to (the place) Italy'.

synecdoche Referring to something by one of its parts (usually the most relevant): e.g. *erant fortasse gladii, sed absconditi nec ita multi* [§108] where *gladii* does duty for 'men armed with swords'

tricolon (crescens), tetracolon A group of three (**tri-**) or four (**tetra-**) members (words, phrases, clauses) in a list; where the last member is longer (**crescens**), a climax is created: e.g. *cur . . . cur . . . cur . . . cur . . . in forum?* [§112]

variatio The avoidance of carelessly and monotonously repeating forms or sentence structures, or ways of approaching a topic: e.g. [§44] The use of questions and statements, Antony's imagined protest; alternating long and short sentences; clothing (*virilem . . . muliebrem togam . . . stolam*) developed into a metaphor for Antony's change of status.

zeugma Where one word (verb or noun) governs two or more others, with differing appropriateness though not to play on words (cf **syllepsis**) – the effect can be one of surprise: e.g. *studiorum . . . non libidinum deversorium* [§104], where *deversorium* is not appropriate for *studiorum* but is for *libidinum*.

Clausulae

[The list below is taken from Ramsey's edition.]

You are not expected to identify clausulae yourself, but even a cursory acquaintance with them adds to the appreciation of what Cicero is doing.

In the following patterns, the normal rules of verse scansion apply to the weight of syllables (heavy –, or light ∪, 'x' for either) and their elision. Metrical patterns that occur in verse are avoided. The last syllable can always be either heavy or light. The five types shown are those by Cicero favoured at the period of the Philippics. For each type

are also given the variations which are created by resolution (where a
– becomes ∪ ∪), substitution (where a – becomes a ∪), or extension
(where an extra metrical unit is tacked on the front:

Type 1:	**cretic + trochee**	– ∪ – – x	-ssisse dicebat [45]
	[resolved first heavy]	∪ ∪ ∪ – – x	sed etiam lucem [87]
	[resolved second heavy]	– ∪ ∪ ∪ – x	exsilium iturum [45]
	[resolved first and second heavy]	∪ ∪ ∪ ∪ ∪ – x	*facere potuisse [2.5]* – not in our extract
	[resolved second and third heavy]	– ∪ ∪ ∪ ∪ ∪ x	*non facere potuit [1.17]* – not in our extract
	[resolved third heavy]	– ∪ – ∪ ∪ x	esse dissimilis [92]
Type 2:	**double cretic**	– ∪ – – ∪ x	-issimis dicere [45]
	[resolved first heavy]	∪ ∪ ∪ – – ∪ x	-a peregrinatio [100]
	[substituted first light]	– – – – ∪ x	-um deversorium [104]
Type 3:	**double trochee**	– ∪ – x	ausus esses [46]
	[molossus + 2 trochees]	– – – – ∪ – x	-us armati obsiderent [89]
	[cretic + 2 trochees]	– ∪ – – ∪ – x	Martias consulatum [82]
	[dactyl + 2 trochees]	– ∪ ∪ – ∪ – x	-or tam humilis, tam abiectus [82]
	[choriamb + 2 trochees]	– ∪ ∪ – – ∪ – x	-o stabili et conlocavit [44]
Type 4:	**cretic + iamb**	– ∪ – ∪ x	-fende si potes [112]
	[substituted first light]	– – – ∪ x	-et defenderem [45]
Type 5:	double **spondee**	– – – x	commendabat [45]
	[cretic + 2 spondees]	– ∪ – – – – x	non suo decoxisset [44]

It is true that many routine sentences end in clausulae – here they imply a deceleration, like semi-colons and full stops which, in Roman times, did not exist. Imposing sentences, too, really need an imposing conclusion and this is what a clausula provides, particularly because it invites a certain relish in delivery. The notes identify several of the clausulae occurring at such points. If you read the clausulae out loud in context, you will find that a majority of heavy syllables contributes to a solid landing – or of light syllables to a soft landing.

Further Reading

Craig, C., 'Audience Expectations, Invective and Proof', in Powell J. and Paterson J., eds., *Cicero the Advocate* (Oxford, 2004) – although focusing on judicial oratory, still sheds light on the political arena.

Denniston, J. D., ed., *Cicero Philippics I & II* (1926 – reprinted Bristol Classical Press, 2013) – a very fine older commentary.

Hall, J., 'Saviour of the Republic and Father of the Fatherland' in C. Steel, ed., *The Cambridge Companion to Cicero* (Cambridge, 2013) – on how Cicero measured up to political crisis.

Harris, R., *Dictator* (Hutchinson, 2015) – a fictional account of Cicero's last years that offers an enjoyable entry into their complexities.

Lausberg, H., *Handbook of Literary Rhetoric* (Brill, 1998) – no reference work on (classical) rhetoric could be more comprehensive, but it is unfortunately not readily available.

Morstein-Marx, R., *Mass Oratory and Political Power in the Late Roman Republic* (Cambridge, 2004) – a detailed analysis of the relationship between oratory and political power at the time.

Ramsey, J. T., ed., *Cicero Philippics I–II* (Cambridge, 2003) – the most recent edition available.

Tempest, K., *Cicero: Politics and Persuasion in Ancient Rome* (Bloomsbury, 2011) – an accessible biography that puts the speeches in their historical and political context.

Maps

Map 1 The Roman World in 50 BC

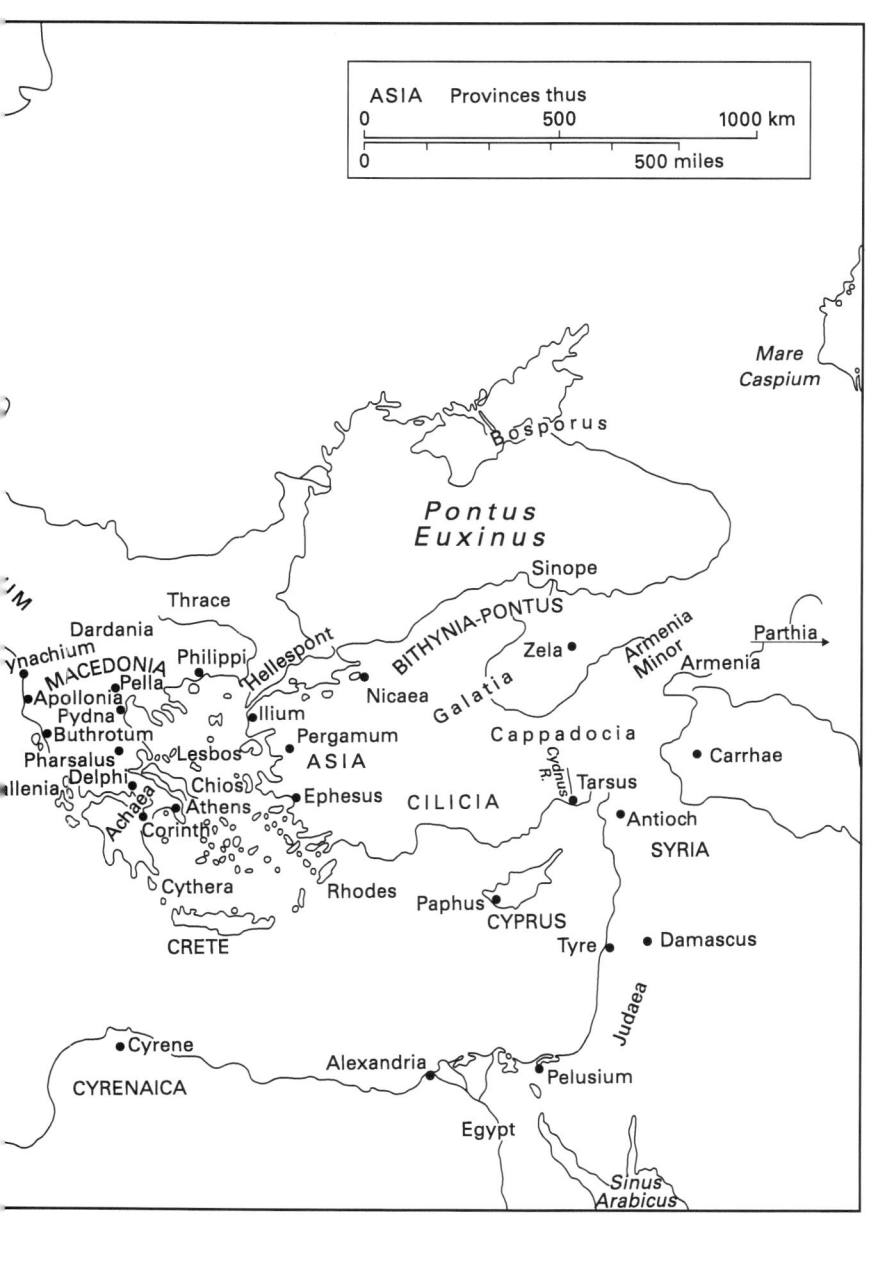

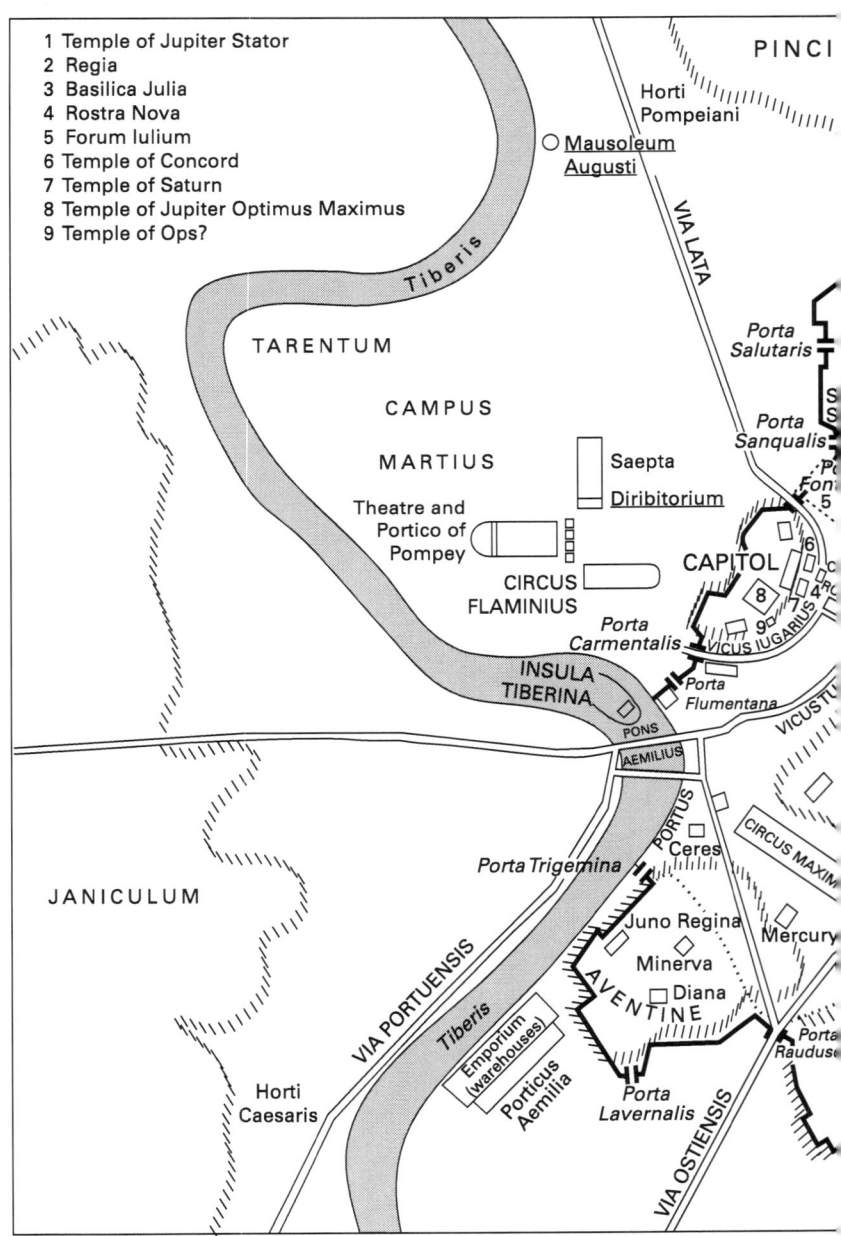

Map 2 Rome in the Late Republic (underlining denotes, later, imperial structures)

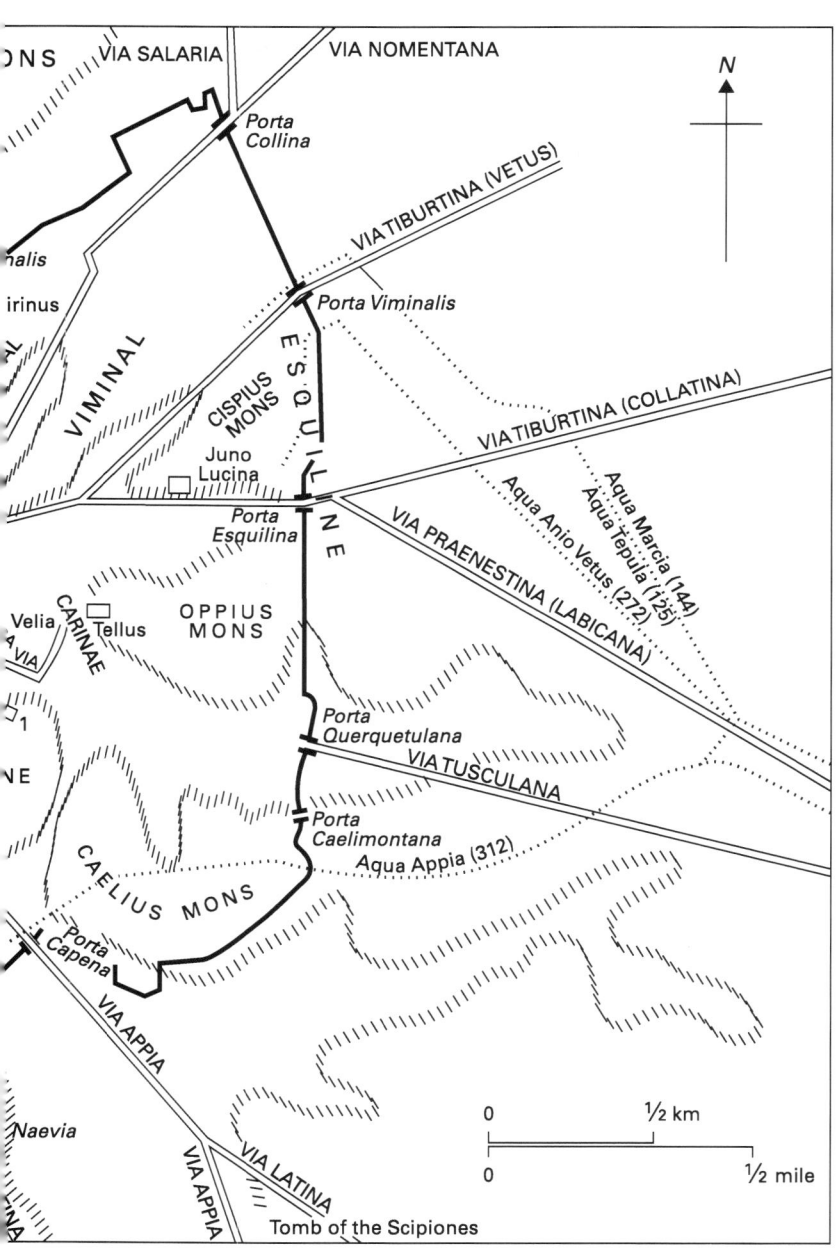

A Note on the Text

The only change, other than punctuation, to Clark's Oxford Classical Text (2nd edition 1918) is at the end of § 91: *dictatorem* for *dictatoris*.

Text

1–43: Cicero begins by repudiating the account of his career that Antony gave in a virulent address to the senate when Cicero himself was absent. He then proceeds to pay Antony back, with interest.

44. XVIII. visne igitur te inspiciamus a puero? sic opinor; a principio ordiamur. tenesne memoria praetextatum te decoxisse? 'patris', inquies, 'ista culpa est'. concedo. etenim est pietatis plena defensio. illud tamen audaciae tuae quod sedisti in quattuordecim ordinibus, cum esset lege Roscia decoctoribus certus locus constitutus, quamvis quis fortunae vitio, non suo decoxisset. sumpsisti virilem, quam statim muliebrem togam reddidisti. primo volgare scortum; certa flagitii merces nec ea parva; sed cito Curio intervenit qui te a meretricio quaestu abduxit et, tamquam stolam dedisset, in matrimonio stabili et certo collocavit.

45. nemo umquam puer emptus libidinis causa tam fuit in domini potestate quam tu in Curionis. quotiens te pater eius domu sua eiecit, quotiens custodes posuit ne limen intrares! cum tu tamen nocte socia, hortante libidine, cogente mercede, per tegulas demittererе. quae flagitia domus illa diutius ferre non potuit. scisne me de rebus mihi notissimis dicere? recordare tempus illud, cum pater Curio maerens iacebat in lecto, filius se ad pedes meos prosternens, lacrimans, te mihi commendabat; orabat ut se contra suum patrem, si sestertium sexagiens peteret, defenderem; tantum enim se pro te intercessisse dicebat. ipse autem amore ardens confirmabat, quod desiderium tui discidi ferre non posset, se in exilium iturum.

46. quo tempore ego quanta mala florentissimae familiae sedavi vel potius sustuli! patri persuasi, ut aes alienum fili dissolveret; redimeret adulescentem summa spe et animi et ingenii praeditum, rei familiaris facultatibus eumque non modo tua familiaritate, sed etiam congressione patrio iure et potestate prohiberet. haec tu cum per me acta meminisses, nisi illis quos videmus gladiis confideres, maledictis me provocare ausus esses?

47. XIX. sed iam stupra et flagitia omittamus: sunt quaedam quae honeste non possum dicere; tu autem eo liberior quod ea in te admisisti quae a verecundo inimico audire non posses. sed reliquum vitae cursum videte, quem quidem celeriter perstringam. ad haec enim, quae in civili bello, in maximis rei publicae miseriis fecit, et ad ea, quae cotidie facit, festinat animus. quae peto ut, quamquam multo notiora vobis quam mihi sunt, tamen, ut facitis, attente audiatis. debet enim talibus in rebus excitare animos non cognitio solum rerum sed etiam recordatio; etsi incidamus, opinor, media ne nimis sero ad extrema veniamus.

48. intimus erat in tribunatu Clodio qui sua erga me beneficia commemorat; eius omnium incendiorum fax, cuius etiam domi iam tum quiddam molitus est. quid dicam ipse optime intellegit. inde iter Alexandream contra senatus auctoritatem, contra rem publicam et religiones; sed habebat ducem Gabinium, quicum quidvis rectissime facere posset. qui tum inde reditus aut qualis? prius in ultimam Galliam ex Aegypto quam domum. quae autem domus? suam enim quisque domum tum obtinebat nec erat usquam tua. domum dico? quid erat in terris ubi in tuo pedem poneres praeter unum Misenum quod cum sociis tamquam Sisaponem tenebas?

49. XX. venis e Gallia ad quaesturam petendam. aude dicere te prius ad parentem tuam venisse quam ad me. acceperam iam ante Caesaris litteras ut mihi satis fieri paterer a te: itaque ne loqui quidem sum te passus de gratia. postea sum cultus a te, tu a me observatus in petitione quaesturae; quo quidem tempore P. Clodium approbante populo Romano in foro es conatus occidere, cumque eam rem tua sponte conarere, non impulsu meo, tamen ita praedicabas, te non existimare, nisi illum interfecisses, umquam mihi pro tuis in me iniuriis satis esse facturum. in quo demiror cur Milonem impulsu meo rem illam egisse dicas, cum te ultro mihi idem illud deferentem numquam sim adhortatus. quamquam, si in eo perseverares, ad tuam gloriam rem illam referri malebam quam ad meam gratiam.

50. quaestor es factus; deinde continuo sine senatus consulto, sine sorte, sine lege ad Caesarem cucurristi. id enim unum in terris egestatis, aeris alieni, nequitiae perditis vitae rationibus, perfugium esse ducebas. ibi te cum et illius largitionibus et tuis rapinis explevisses, si hoc est explere, expilare quod statim effundas, advolasti egens ad tribunatum, ut in eo magistratu, si posses, viri tui similis esses.

50b-78a: Cicero moves on to Antony's deeds as tribunus plebis and his contribution to Caesar's march on Rome; how he became Caesar's magister equitum (deputy) at Pharsalus; and how, over this period, he displayed a mixture of opportunism, greed, profligacy and treachery. Cicero even suggests that Antony, to excape paying what he owed, sent an assassin to Caesar's house the day before Caesar set off to take on the remainder of the Pompeian forces in Spain – a war in which Antony took no part.

XXXII. C. Caesari ex Hispania redeunti obviam longissime processisti. celeriter isti, redisti, ut cognosceret te si minus fortem, at tamen strenuum. factus es ei rursus nescio quo modo familiaris. habebat hoc omnino Caesar: quem plane perditum aere alieno egentemque, si eundem nequam hominem audacemque cognorat, hunc in familiaritatem libentissime recipiebat.

79. his igitur rebus praeclare commendatus iussus es renuntiari consul et quidem cum ipso. nihil queror de Dolabella qui tum est impulsus, inductus, elusus. qua in re quanta fuerit uterque vestrum perfidia in Dolabellam, quis ignorat? ille induxit ut peteret, promissum et receptum intervertit ad seque transtulit; tu eius perfidiae voluntatem tuam ascripsisti. veniunt Kalendae Ianuariae; cogimur in senatum: invectus est copiosius multo in istum et paratius Dolabella quam nunc ego.

80. hic autem iratus quae dixit, di boni! primum cum Caesar ostendisset se, prius quam proficisceretur, Dolabellam consulem esse iussurum — quem negant regem, qui et faceret semper eius modi aliquid et diceret — sed cum Caesar ita dixisset, tum hic bonus augur eo se sacerdotio praeditum esse dixit ut comitia auspiciis vel impedire vel vitiare posset, idque se facturum esse adseveravit. in quo primum incredibilem stupiditatem hominis cognoscite.

81. quid enim? istud, quod te sacerdoti iure facere posse dixisti, si augur non esses et consul esses, minus facere potuisses? vide ne etiam facilius. nos enim nuntiationem solum habemus, consules et reliqui magistratus etiam spectionem. esto: hoc imperite; nec enim est ab homine numquam sobrio postulanda prudentia, sed videte impudentiam. multis ante mensibus in senatu dixit se Dolabellae comitia aut prohibiturum auspiciis aut id facturum esse quod fecit. quisquamne divinare potest quid viti in auspiciis futurum sit, nisi qui de caelo servare constituit? quod neque licet comitiis per leges et si qui servavit non comitiis habitis, sed priusquam habeantur, debet nuntiare. verum implicata inscientia impudentia est: nec scit quod augurem nec facit quod pudentem decet.

82. atque ex illo die recordamini eius usque ad Idus Martias consulatum. quis umquam apparitor tam humilis, tam abiectus? nihil ipse poterat; omnia rogabat; caput in aversam lecticam inserens, beneficia quae venderet a conlega petebat. ecce Dolabellae comitiorum dies.

XXXIII. sortitio praerogativae; quiescit. renuntiatur: tacet. prima classis vocatur, deinde ita ut adsolet suffragia, tum secunda classis vocatur, quae omnia sunt citius facta quam dixi.

83. confecto negotio bonus augur — C. Laelium diceres — 'Alio die' inquit. o impudentiam singularem! quid videras, quid senseras, quid audieras? neque enim te de caelo servasse dixisti nec hodie dicis. id igitur obvenit vitium quod tu iam Kalendis Ianuariis futurum esse provideras et tanto ante praedixeras. ergo hercule magna, ut spero, tua potius quam rei publicae calamitate ementitus es auspicia; obstrinxisti religione populum Romanum; augur auguri, consul consuli obnuntiasti. nolo plura, ne acta Dolabellae videar convellere, quae necesse est aliquando ad nostrum conlegium deferantur.

84. sed adrogantiam hominis insolentiamque cognoscite. quam diu tu voles, vitiosus consul Dolabella; rursus, cum voles, salvis auspiciis creatus. si nihil est, cum augur eis verbis nuntiat, quibus tu nuntiasti, confitere te, cum 'Alio die' dixeris, sobrium non fuisse; sin est aliqua vis in istis verbis, ea quae sit augur a conlega requiro. sed ne forte ex multis rebus gestis M. Antoni rem unam pulcherrimam transiliat oratio, ad Lupercalia veniamus.

XXXIV. non dissimulat, patres conscripti: apparet esse commotum; sudat, pallet. quidlibet, modo ne nauseet, faciat quod in porticu Minucia fecit. quae potest esse turpitudinis tantae defensio? cupio audire, ut videam ubi rhetoris sit tanta merces, ubi campus Leontinus appareat.

85. sedebat in rostris conlega tuus amictus toga purpurea, in sella aurea, coronatus. escendis, accedis ad sellam — ita eras Lupercus ut te consulem esse meminisse deberes — diadema ostendis. gemitus toto foro. unde diadema? non enim abiectum sustuleras, sed attuleras domo meditatum et cogitatum scelus. tu diadema imponebas cum plangore populi; ille cum plausu reiciebat. tu ergo unus, scelerate, inventus es qui cum auctor regni esses, eumque quem conlegam habebas dominum habere velles, idem temptares quid populus Romanus ferre et pati posset.

86. at etiam misericordiam captabas: supplex te ad pedes abiciebas. quid petens? ut servires? tibi uni peteres qui ita a puero vixeras ut omnia paterere, ut facile servires; a nobis populoque Romano mandatum id certe non habebas. o praeclaram illam eloquentiam tuam, cum es nudus contionatus! quid hoc turpius, quid foedius, quid suppliciis omnibus dignius? num exspectas dum te stimulis fodiamus? haec te, si ullam partem habes sensus, lacerat, haec cruentat oratio. vereor ne imminuam summorum virorum gloriam; dicam tamen dolore commotus: quid indignius quam vivere eum qui imposuerit diadema, cum omnes fateantur iure interfectum esse qui abiecerit?

87. at etiam ascribi iussit in fastis ad Lupercalia: C. Caesari, dictatori perpetuo, M. Antonium consulem populi iussu regnum detulisse; Caesarem uti noluisse. iam iam minime miror te otium perturbare; non modo urbem odisse, sed etiam lucem; cum perditissimis latronibus non solum de die, sed etiam in diem bibere. ubi enim tu in pace consistes? qui locus tibi in legibus et in iudiciis esse potest, quae tu, quantum in te fuit, dominatu regio sustulisti? ideone L. Tarquinius exactus, Sp. Cassius, Sp. Maelius, M. Manlius necati ut multis post saeculis a M. Antonio, quod fas non est, rex Romae constitueretur?

88. XXXV. sed ad auspicia redeamus, de quibus Idibus Martiis fuit in senatu Caesar acturus. quaero: tum tu quid egisses? audiebam equidem te paratum venisse, quod me de ementitis auspiciis, quibus tamen parere necesse erat, putares esse dicturum. sustulit illum diem fortuna rei publicae. num etiam tuum de auspiciis iudicium interitus Caesaris sustulit? sed incidi in id tempus quod iis rebus in quas ingressa erat oratio praevertendum est. quae tua fuga, quae formido praeclaro illo die, quae propter conscientiam scelerum desperatio vitae, cum ex illa fuga beneficio eorum qui te, si sanus esses, salvum esse voluerunt, clam te domum recepisti!

89. o mea frustra semper verissima auguria rerum futurarum! dicebam illis in Capitolio liberatoribus nostris, cum me ad te ire vellent, ut ad defendendam rem publicam te adhortarer, quoad metueres, omnia te promissurum; simul ac timere desisses, similem te futurum tui. itaque cum ceteri consulares irent, redirent, in sententia mansi: neque te illo die neque postero vidi neque ullam societatem optimis civibus cum importunissimo hoste foedere ullo confirmari posse credidi. post diem tertium veni in aedem Telluris et quidem invitus, cum omnes aditus armati obsiderent.

90. qui tibi dies ille, M. Antoni, fuit! quamquam mihi inimicus subito exstitisti, tamen me tui miseret, quod tibi invideris.

XXXVI. qui tu vir, di immortales, et quantus fuisses, si illius diei mentem servare potuisses! pacem haberemus, quae erat facta per obsidem puerum nobilem, M. Bambalionis nepotem. quamquam bonum te timor faciebat, non diuturnus magister officii, improbum fecit ea quae, dum timor abest, a te non discedit, audacia. etsi tum, cum optimum te putabant me quidem dissentiente, funeri tyranni, si illud funus fuit, sceleratissime praefuisti.

91. tua illa pulchra laudatio, tua miseratio, tua cohortatio; tu, tu, inquam, illas faces incendisti, et eas, quibus semustilatus ille est et eas quibus incensa L. Bellieni domus deflagravit. tu illos impetus perditorum hominum et ex maxima parte servorum quos nos vi manuque reppulimus in nostras domos immisisti. idem tamen quasi fuligine abstersa reliquis diebus in Capitolio praeclara senatus consulta fecisti, ne qua post Idus Martias immunitatis tabula neve cuius benefici figeretur. meministi ipse de exsulibus, scis de immunitate quid dixeris. optimum vero quod dictaturae nomen in perpetuum de re publica sustulisti: quo quidem facto tantum te cepisse odium regni videbatur ut eius omnem propter proximum dictatorem metum tolleres.

92. constituta res publica videbatur aliis, mihi vero nullo modo, qui omnia te gubernante naufragia metuebam. num igitur me fefellit, aut num diutius sui potuit esse dissimilis? inspectantibus vobis toto Capitolio tabulae figebantur, neque solum singulis venibant immunitates, sed etiam populis universis: civitas non iam singillatim, sed provinciis totis dabatur. itaque si haec manent quae stante re publica manere non possunt, provincias universas, patres conscripti, perdidistis, neque vectigalia solum, sed etiam imperium populi Romani huius domesticis nundinis deminutum est.

93–99: Cicero turns to the vast amounts of money that Antony suddenly acquired – by appropriating the contents of the treasury in the temple of Ops, where Caesar had stashed his fund for the imminent war against the Parthians; and, more peacemeal, by claiming decisions of his own – lucrative gifts of territory or citizenship – to be Caesar's: Antony had privileged access to Caesar's private papers. Yet this largesse did not include Antony's restoring the fortunes of his exiled uncle.

100. XXXIX. sed ad chirographa redeamus. quae tua fuit cognitio? acta enim Caesaris pacis causa confirmata sunt a senatu: quae quidem Caesar egisset, non ea quae egisse Caesarem dixisset Antonius. unde ista erumpunt, quo auctore proferuntur? si sunt falsa, cur probantur? si vera, cur veneunt? at sic placuerat, ut ex Kalendis Iuniis de Caesaris actis cum consilio cognosceretis. quod fuit consilium, quem umquam convocasti, quas Kalendas Iunias exspectasti? an eas ad quas te peragratis veteranorum coloniis stipatum armis rettulisti? o praeclaram illam percursationem tuam mense Aprili atque Maio, tum cum etiam Capuam coloniam deducere conatus es! quem ad modum illinc abieris vel potius paene non abieris scimus.

101. cui tu urbi minitaris. utinam conere, ut aliquando illud 'paene' tollatur! at quam nobilis est tua illa peregrinatio! quid prandiorum apparatus, quid furiosam vinulentiam tuam proferam?

tua ista detrimenta sunt, illa nostra: agrum Campanum, qui cum de vectigalibus eximebatur ut militibus daretur, tamen infligi magnum rei publicae vulnus putabamus, hunc tu compransoribus tuis et conlusoribus dividebas. mimos dico et mimas, patres conscripti, in agro Campano collocatos. quid iam querar de agro Leontino? quoniam quidem hae quondam arationes Campana et Leontina in populi Romani patrimonio grandiferae et fructuosae ferebantur. medico tria milia iugerum: quid, si te sanasset? rhetori duo; quid, si te disertum facere potuisset? sed ad iter Italiamque redeamus.

102. XL. deduxisti coloniam Casilinum, quo Caesar ante deduxerat. consuluisti me per litteras de Capua tu quidem, sed idem de Casilino respondissem: possesne, ubi colonia esset, eo coloniam novam iure deducere. negavi in eam coloniam quae esset auspicato deducta, dum esset incolumis, coloniam novam iure deduci: colonos novos ascribi posse rescripsi. tu autem insolentia elatus omni auspiciorum iure turbato Casilinum coloniam deduxisti, quo erat paucis annis ante deducta, ut vexillum tolleres, ut aratrum circumduceres; cuius quidem vomere portam Capuae paene perstrinxisti, ut florentis coloniae territorium minueretur.

103. ab hac perturbatione religionum advolas in M. Varronis, sanctissimi atque integerrimi viri, fundum Casinatem. quo iure, quo ore? 'eodem', inquies, 'quo in heredum L. Rubri, quo in heredum L. Turseli praedia, quo in reliquas innumerabiles possessiones.' et si ab hasta, valeat hasta, valeant tabulae modo Caesaris, non tuae, quibus debuisti, non quibus tu te liberavisti. Varronis quidem Casinatem fundum quis venisse dicit, quis hastam istius venditionis vidit, quis vocem praeconis audivit? misisse te dicis Alexandream qui emeret a Caesare; ipsum enim exspectare magnum fuit.

104. quis vero audivit umquam – nullius autem salus curae pluribus fuit – de fortunis Varronis rem ullam esse detractam? quid? si etiam scripsit ad te Caesar ut redderes, quid satis potest dici de tanta impudentia? remove gladios parumper illos quos videmus: iam intelleges aliam causam esse hastae Caesaris, aliam confidentiae et temeritatis tuae. non enim te dominus modo illis sedibus, sed quivis amicus, vicinus, hospes, procurator arcebit.

XLI. at quam multos dies in ea villa turpissime es perbacchatus! ab hora tertia bibebatur, ludebatur, vomebatur. o tecta ipsa misera, 'quam dispari domino' – quamquam quo modo iste dominus? – sed tamen quam ab dispari tenebantur! studiorum enim suorum M. Varro voluit illud, non libidinum deversorium.

105. quae in illa villa antea dicebantur, quae cogitabantur, quae litteris mandabantur! iura populi Romani, monumenta maiorum, omnis sapientiae ratio omnisque doctrinae. at vero te inquilino – non enim domino – personabant omnia vocibus ebriorum, natabant pavimenta vino, madebant parietes, ingenui pueri cum meritoriis, scorta inter matres familias versabantur. Casino salutatum veniebant, Aquino, Interamna; admissus est nemo. iure id quidem; in homine enim turpissimo obsolefiebant dignitatis insignia.

106. cum inde Romam proficiscens ad Aquinum accederet, obviam ei processit, ut est frequens municipium, magna sane multitudo. at iste operta lectica latus per oppidum est ut mortuus. stulte Aquinates; sed tamen in via habitabant. quid Anagnini? qui cum essent devii, descenderunt, ut istum, tamquam si esset consul, salutarent. incredibile dictu, sed inter omnes constabat neminem esse resalutatum, praesertim cum duos secum Anagninos haberet, Mustelam et Laconem, quorum alter gladiorum est princeps, alter poculorum.

107. quid ego illas istius minas contumeliasque commemorem quibus invectus est in Sidicinos, vexavit Puteolanos, quod C. Cassium et Brutos patronos adoptassent? magno quidem studio, iudicio, benevolentia, caritate, non, ut te et Basilum, vi et armis, et alios vestri similes quos clientes nemo habere velit, non modo illorum cliens esse.

XLII. interea dum tu abes, qui dies ille conlegae tui fuit, cum illud quod venerari solebas bustum in foro evertit! qua re tibi nuntiata, ut constabat inter eos qui una fuerunt concidisti. quid evenerit postea nescio – metum credo valuisse et arma – conlegam quidem de caelo detraxisti effecistique non tu quidem etiam nunc ut similis tui, sed certe ut dissimilis esset sui.

108. qui vero inde reditus Romam, quae perturbatio totius urbis! memineramus Cinnam nimis potentem, Sullam postea dominantem, modo Caesarem regnantem videramus. erant fortasse gladii, sed absconditi nec ita multi. Ista vero quae et quanta barbaria est! agmine quadrato cum gladiis sequuntur, scutorum lecticas portari videmus. atque his quidem iam inveteratis, patres conscripti, consuetudine obduruimus. Kalendis Iuniis cum in senatum, ut erat constitutum, venire vellemus, metu perterriti repente diffugimus.

109. at iste, qui senatu non egeret, neque desideravit quemquam et potius discessu nostro laetatus est statimque illa mirabilia facinora effecit. qui chirographa Caesaris defendisset lucri sui causa, is leges Caesaris, easque praeclaras, ut rem publicam concutere posset, evertit. numerum annorum provinciis prorogavit; idemque, cum actorum Caesaris defensor esse deberet, et in publicis et in privatis rebus acta Caesaris rescidit. in publicis nihil est lege gravius; in privatis firmissimum est testamentum. leges alias sine promulgatione sustulit, alias ut tolleret promulgavit. testamentum irritum fecit, quod etiam infimis civibus semper obtentum est. signa, tabulas, quas populo Caesar una cum hortis legavit, eas hic partim in hortos Pompei deportavit, partim in villam Scipionis.

110. XLIII. et tu in Caesaris memoria diligens, tu illum amas mortuum? quem is honorem maiorem consecutus erat quam ut haberet pulvinar, simulacrum, fastigium, flaminem? est ergo flamen, ut Iovi, ut Marti, ut Quirino, sic divo Iulio M. Antonius. quid igitur cessas? cur non inaugeraris? sume diem, vide qui te inauguret: conlegae sumus; nemo negabit. o detestabilem hominem, sive quod tyranni sacerdos es sive quod mortui! quaero deinceps num hodiernus dies qui sit ignores. nescis heri quartum in circo diem ludorum Romanorum fuisse? te autem ipsum ad populum tulisse, ut quintus praeterea dies Caesari tribueretur? cur non sumus praetextati? cur honorem Caesaris tua lege datum deseri patimur? an supplicationes addendo diem contaminari passus es, pulvinaria noluisti? aut undique religionem tolle aut usque quaque conserva.

111. quaeris placeatne mihi pulvinar esse, fastigium, flaminem. mihi vero nihil istorum placet sed tu qui acta Caesaris defendis quid potes dicere cur alia defendas, alia non cures? nisi forte vis fateri te omnia quaestu tuo, non illius dignitate metiri. quid ad haec tandem? exspecto enim eloquentiam. disertissimum cognovi avum tuum, at te etiam apertiorem in dicendo. ille numquam nudus est contionatus; tuum hominis simplicis pectus vidimus. respondebisne ad haec, aut omnino hiscere audebis? ecquid reperies ex tam longa oratione mea cui te respondere posse confidas?

112. XLIV. sed praeterita omittamus: hunc unum diem, unum, inquam, hodiernum diem, hoc punctum temporis, quo loquor, defende, si potes. cur armatorum corona senatus saeptus est, cur me tui satellites cum gladiis audiunt, cur valvae Concordiae non patent, cur homines omnium gentium maxime barbaros, Ituraeos, cum sagittis deducis in forum? praesidi sui causa se facere dicit. non igitur miliens perire est melius quam in sua civitate sine armatorum praesidio non posse vivere? sed nullum est istuc, mihi crede, praesidium: caritate te et benivolentia civium saeptum oportet esse, non armis.

113. eripiet et extorquebit tibi ista populus Romanus, utinam salvis nobis! sed quoquo modo nobiscum egeris, dum istis consiliis uteris, non potes, mihi crede, esse diuturnus. etenim ista tua minime avara coniunx quam ego sine contumelia describo nimium diu debet populo Romano tertiam pensionem. habet populus Romanus ad quos gubernacula rei publicae deferat: qui ubicumque terrarum sunt, ibi omne est rei publicae praesidium vel potius ipsa res publica, quae se adhuc tantum modo ulta est, nondum recuperavit. habet quidem certe res publica adulescentes nobilissimos paratos defensores. quam volent illi cedant otio consulentes; tamen a re publica revocabuntur. et nomen pacis dulce est et ipsa res salutaris; sed inter pacem et servitutem plurimum interest. pax est tranquilla libertas, servitus postremum malorum omnium, non modo bello sed morte etiam repellendum.

114. quod si se ipsos illi nostri liberatores e conspectu nostro abstulerunt, at exemplum facti reliquerunt. illi quod nemo fecerat fecerunt. Tarquinium Brutus bello est persecutus, qui tum rex fuit cum esse Romae licebat; Sp. Cassius, Sp. Maelius, M. Manlius propter suspicionem regni appetendi sunt necati: hi primum cum gladiis non in regnum appetentem, sed in regnantem impetum fecerunt. quod cum ipsum factum per se praeclarum est atque divinum, tum expositum ad imitandum est, praesertim cum illi eam gloriam consecuti sint quae vix caelo capi posse videatur. etsi enim satis in ipsa conscientia pulcherrimi facti fructus erat, tamen mortali immortalitatem non arbitror esse contemnendam.

115. XLV. recordare igitur illum, M. Antoni, diem quo dictaturam sustulisti; pone ante oculos laetitiam senatus populique Romani; confer cum hac nundinatione tua tuorumque: tum intelleges quantum inter laudem et lucrum intersit. sed nimirum, ut quidam morbo aliquo et sensus stupore suavitatem cibi non sentiunt, sic libidinosi, avari, facinerosi verae laudis gustatum non habent. sed si te laus adlicere ad recte faciendum non potest, ne metus quidem a foedissimis factis potest avocare? iudicia non metuis: si propter innocentiam, laudo; sin propter vim, non intellegis, qui isto modo iudicia non timeat, ei quid timendum sit?

116. quod si non metuis viros fortes egregiosque cives, quod a corpore tuo prohibentur armis, tui te, mihi crede, diutius non ferent. quae est autem vita dies et noctes timere a suis? nisi vero aut maioribus habes beneficiis obligatos quam ille quosdam habuit ex iis a quibus est interfectus, aut tu es ulla re cum eo comparandus. fuit in illo ingenium, ratio, memoria, litterae, cura, cogitatio, diligentia; res bello gesserat, quamvis rei publicae calamitosas, at tamen magnas; multos annos regnare meditatus, magno labore, magnis periculis, quod cogitarat effecerat; muneribus, monumentis, congiariis, epulis multitudinem imperitam delenierat; suos praemiis, adversarios clementiae specie devinxerat. quid multa? attulerat iam liberae civitati partim metu, partim patientia consuetudinem serviendi.

117. XLVI. cum illo ego te dominandi cupiditate conferre possum, ceteris vero rebus nullo modo comparandus es. sed ex plurimis malis quae ab illo rei publicae sunt inusta hoc tamen boni est quod didicit iam populus Romanus quantum cuique crederet, quibus se committeret, a quibus caveret. haec non cogitas, neque intellegis satis esse viris fortibus didicisse quam sit re pulchrum, beneficio gratum, fama gloriosum tyrannum occidere? an, cum illum homines non tulerint, te ferent?

118. certatim posthac, mihi crede, ad hoc opus curretur neque occasionis tarditas exspectabitur. respice, quaeso, aliquando rem publicam, M. Antoni, quibus ortus sis, non quibuscum vivas, considera: mecum, ut voles: redi cum re publica in gratiam. sed de te tu videris; ego de me ipse profitebor. defendi rem publicam adulescens, non deseram senex: contempsi Catilinae gladios, non pertimescam tuos.

quin etiam corpus libenter obtulerim, si repraesentari morte mea libertas civitatis potest, ut aliquando dolor populi Romani pariat quod iam diu parturit!

119. etenim, si abhinc annos prope viginti hoc ipso in templo negavi posse mortem immaturam esse consulari, quanto verius nunc negabo seni? mihi vero, patres conscripti, iam etiam optanda mors est perfuncto rebus iis quas adeptus sum quasque gessi. duo modo haec opto, unum ut moriens populum Romanum liberum relinquam – hoc mihi maius ab dis immortalibus dari nihil potest – alterum ut ita cuique eveniat ut de re publica quisque mereatur.

Commentary Notes

In the notes on language, '**NLG**...' designates a paragraph in Bennett's New Latin Grammar (by Charles E. Bennett, 1895), available online at several web addresses. Asterisked terms are explained in the final sections of 'Introduction – Oratory'. Two abbreviations might be unfamiliar: 'sc.' (*scilicet*, 'supply this missing word or words') and 'cf.' (*confer*, 'compare with'). Where references are made to 'style notes', these are to be found online, at www.bloomsbury.com/bloomsbury-classical-languages, where a summary of the parts of the speech not on the syllabus is also given.

Where the chapter number below is followed by a letter, 'a' designates the first paragraph, 'b' the second. Phrases underlined indicate the main topic of a particular section.

> **Exordium** (sections 1–2): Over the last twenty years, every enemy of the Republic has declared war on me. Why is Antony now doing this? Contempt? Because the Senate is a sympathetic audience? Because he fancies his chances in debate? Ultimately it must be because this is the best way for him to prove himself an enemy of his country.
>
> **Tractatio** (sections 3–114):
>
> **Narratio** omitted (see 'Introduction – Oratory)
>
> **Confutatio** (sections 3–43):
>
> Sections 3–10a: Antony has accused me of breaching our friendship by at some point appearing in court against one of his connections. But I was representing a close friend of my own against a stranger. Antony claims he gave up his candidacy for the augurship for my benefit. But I was sought out by the college of augurs. Antony pretends to have done me a great kindness, presumably when he spared my life at Brundisium,

But how could he have opposed the ordinance of Caesar himself? Antony read out a letter from me as evidence of my esteem [*ad Att.,* 14.13 b – in which Cicero agrees, with queasy unctuousness, to Antony's request for the recall of Sextus Cloelius]. Apart from showing his lack of respect for civilised values and the privacy of the mails, he also establishes his own folly, as it is evidence of no more than that I once wrote to him, who is now an outlaw, as if he were a fellow-citizen and decent man.

[**Divisio** (section 10b): I will speak first in my defence and then against Antony. Although I have been known throughout my career for the decorum with which I speak, do not be surprised if I respond to Antony in the manner which he has himself invited.]

Sections 11–20: Antony reproaches me with my consulship [63 BC, the year of the Catilinarian conspiracy...], as though I had acted in my own name and not that of the Senate. But nobody except you and P. Clodius has denounced my consulship; and the list of those it pleased is long and distinguished, including Pompey himself. Still alive are L. Cotta, who decreed a thanksgiving for what I did, and Antony's uncle, L. Caesar, who spoke in favour of the execution of his own brother-in-law, your stepfather. And you, who ringed the temple of Concord with guards [on 19th September 44 BC] dare to accuse me of packing the Capitoline Hill with armed slaves! Then in fact there was an abundance of volunteers from the ranks of the nobles to protect it. And when there was ample proof of the conspirators' destructive ambitions, what leader could have refrained from protecting the common good? At the same time as you admit your stepfather was involved in the conspiracy, you complain that I did not hand over his body for burial – though it was the Senate that punished them. And lastly, you make gibes at my poetry, you who have no appreciation of such matters.

Sections 21–22: Antony asserts that P. Clodius was killed at my instigation. This is a strange charge from a man who himself nearly killed Clodius in a brawl and after the trial of Milo [Clodius's killer] never implicated me in the crime.

Sections 23–24: According to Antony, it was I who, by rupturing the alliance between Pompey and Caesar, caused the outbreak of the Civil War. I admit that, at first, I did my best to sever the relationship – but then Caesar destroyed the friendship between Pompey and me, and thereafter I could have had no effect even if I had wanted to.

Sections 25–36: A new charge that Antony makes is that I urged the assassination of Caesar. Yet I have never been listed among the perpetrators even though their names were made public almost immediately, and with glory. The fact that Brutus raised the bloody dagger and, you claim, invoked the name 'Cicero' shows only that he viewed me, like himself, as a liberator. The fact that I was glad it was done is not to my discredit: all decent men rejoice at Caesar's death; all would have participated, if they could.

Sections 37–40a: In Pompey's camp, Antony maintains I was a source of gloom and despondency, or of bad jokes; but I, rightly as it turned out, foresaw the fall of the Republic and, unlike Pompey, was concerned more with security than present honour. Pompey never ceased to respect my judgement.

Sections 40b–42a: From what Antony says, I received nothing from inheritances. This is simply false. What I have received in inheritances, however, comes from friends, while you appear to inherit from complete strangers, or after the disappearance of other designated heirs.

[**Transitio** (sections 42b–43): All this motley set of points Antony assembled in the villa of Metellus Scipio while drinking with his friends; he had also paid a fortune to a tutor of rhetoric (see §§ 84, 101) to argue in whatever way he wished against him, by way of practice. But, now I have replied sufficiently to what he has said about me, it is my turn to say something – far from everything – about him.]

Confirmatio (sections 44–114): see notes below.

Conclusio (sections 115–119): – see notes below.

Section 44

visne... inspiciamus: inspiciamus is subjunctive after **volo** – 'Do you want us to examine...?' **NLG 296.1.a. a puero** – 'from boyhood', as if to say no more than 'from the beginning' (**a principio**) in the next sentence, but in fact to underscore Antony's far from innocent precocity.

sic opinor: sic is better taken as freestanding, 'yes indeed', in answer to the *rhetorical question, than as qualifying **opinor.**

ordiamur: jussive subjunctive, 'let us start'.

tenesne memoria is followed by an accusative (**te**, with **praetextatum** in agreement with it) and infinitive (**decoxisse**). The *toga praetexta*, a toga bordered with purple to recall the gown worn by the kings of Rome, was what boys wore until, at the age of 15 or 16, they took up the plain white *toga virilis* – as we see in Antony's case, four sentences on. **decoxisse** means literally 'to have boiled down (to nothing)' and for a moment seems to attribute responsibility to the youthful Antony. In fact, his father had left him only debts (see §42,). Sallust (*Histories* 3.3) described this M. Antonius Creticus as *'perdendae pecuniae genitus et vacuus a curis, nisi instantibus'* – 'born to lose money and immune to worries unless they were pressing'.

'patris... est.' inquies is future of *inquam* **NLG 134. patris** is in emphatic position by *hyperbaton. **ista culpa** – 'that fault you are referring to'. Antony is made to admit that he was a bankrupt, even if he denies he brought it on himself.

etenim... defensio – translate as **defensio est plena pietatis**. Cicero's tone is snide.

illud – anticipates **quod**, 'the fact that...' **NLG 299.1.a.**; understand *fuit*, omitted for economy and speed, before **audaciae tuae**, a genitive of quality **NLG 203.5. audacia** is very often a bad quality – not so much 'boldness' as 'rashness', 'impertinence', 'over-assertiveness'. Cicero uses it in particular for enemies of the state. The **tuae** is in antithesis to the earlier **patris**, the idea being 'you can't blame your father for your impudence'.

quattuordecim ordinibus: The fourteen rows immediately behind the orchestra, the area in front of the stage where the senators sat, were reserved under the *lex Roscia* of 67 BC for equestrians. Those who had not met the property qualification for equestrians in the census could be fined for sitting in these seats. No other author, however, refers to the seats Cicero goes on to mention, those specifically allocated to bankrupts.

cum = 'although' **NLG 309.3. decoctoribus** is dative of advantage **NLG 188.1.** depending on **constitutus. quamvis. . . decoxisset: quis** here = 'someone', on the analogy of *si, ne, nisi, num* **NLG 91.5.** – 'Even if someone had gone bankrupt not through his own fault, but that of his bad luck.'

sumpsisti. . . reddidisti: Take **togam** with both **virilem** and **muliebrem** (predicative after **reddidisti**: 'which you turned into a woman's'). For the *toga praetexta* and *toga virilis*, see note earlier in this chapter under *praetextatum*. In the mocking contrast between (**togam**) **virilem** and **muliebrem**, Cicero alludes to the *toga meretricum*, the garment worn by prostitutes who were banned from wearing the Roman matron's **stola**. (To the **stola** Cicero comes in three sentences' time.) Antony was, according to Cicero, a high-class rent-boy: as well as for his venality, Antony incurs contempt for being the passive partner in a homosexual relationship.

primo. . .: Supply *fuisti*. **volgare** comments on the role, not the price – as Cicero quickly clarifies. **scortum** – youthful prostitution was a standard ingredient of invective. **certa. . .**: Again, supply *fuit*.

flagitii – **flagitium** is a word often used for sexual transgressions – Cicero's vocabulary for different forms of misconduct is rich and full of nuance.

Curio: C. Scribonius Curio, *tribunus plebis* in 50 BC and only a year or two older than Antony, is not portrayed by Plutarch (who otherwise follows Cicero) as Antony's lover. Seventeen years earlier Cicero in his letters (*ad Att.* 1.14.5) called him *filiola Curionis*, 'girlish daughter of (the elder) Curio'. **tamquam stolam dedisset: tamquam**, 'as if', governs the subjunctive **dedisset NLG 307**. For **stolam**, see previous note on **muliebrem**. 'As if he had made you his wife.'

Section 45

nemo umquam puer: puer in apposition **NLG 169.1**. to **nemo**. **emptus**: Cicero depicts the relationship with the younger Curio as starting on a fee-paying basis (cf. **mercede**, two sentences on). **in Curionis** – sc. *potestate*.

pater: Curio's father had a name identical to his own – C. Scribonius Curio. He was consul in 76 BC, was a staunch opponent of Caesar and therefore might have been expected to be an ally of Cicero's. Their common interest did not, however, prevent the elder Curio from defending Cicero's arch-enemy P. Clodius at his trial in 61 BC; Cicero wrote a (now fragmentary) pamphlet attacking him along with Clodius, *in P. Clodium et Curionem*. **domu** is an archaic form of the ablative *domo* (given by certain manuscripts). **limen**, literally 'threshold', is not uncommonly used by *synecdoche for the entrance, or even for the whole house.

cum. . . demitterere: A natural enough fragment of a sentence – **cum** could be translated 'whereupon. . .'. **nocte socia** – ablative of attendant circumstances **NLG 221.**, much like an ablative absolute but where an adjective stands in for the participle (there being no present participle from *sum*). It creates a *tricolon crescendo where **socia** moves to **hortante** and then to **cogente** ('friendly... urging... compelling...') – in depiction of Antony's ever more impatient appetite. **demitterere** = *demittereris*, 'you were lowered', or 'you lowered yourself' (like a Greek middle **NLG 256.**

quae flagitia – connecting relative **NLG 251.6.**, 'these scandals'. **domus illa** – Curio's family, the house personified.

recordare – imperative, 'Recall ...'. **cum** + indicative because pinpointing the time at which an event took place **NLG 288.A.1.** **pater Curio** – 'the elder Curio'.

se contra suum patrem... defenderem: The younger Curio, having stood surety for Antony's debts (**intercessisse**), now faced asking (**peteret**) his father to meet them because Antony himself could not, being a *decoctor*. So, the younger Curio is shown abjectly begging Cicero to plead his case with his father. [Some editors read *te*, i.e. Antony, as the object of **defenderem**, on the grounds that the terms **peto** and **defendo** have legal connotations and Curio's father would take Antony to court, not his own son. This would make Cicero's position even more paradoxical, in the context of the Philippics.]

sestertium sexagiens: '6 million sesterces'. Millions in Latin are expressed by '-ie(n)s', meaning '<so many> times', then by *centena milia*, expressed or understood **NLG 79.**, then by the genitive customary after *milia* **NLG 80.5.** – **sestertium** is, in origin at least, an abbreviated form of *sestertiorum* **NLG 25.6.** Thus, the sum is 60 x 100,000 = 6,000,000. Multiples of 30 were often resorted to for impressive large numbers, so this might not be an accurate figure. In 44 BC Antony owed 40 million sesterces (§ 90 below).

tantum: 'Such a massive sum', object of **intercessisse**, 'stood surety for'.

quod... posset: Subjunctive after **quod** because part of what Curio said NLG 314.1. **desiderium tui discidi** – **desiderium** amounts to 'pain'; **discidi** is genitive (for *discidii*) NLG 25.2. – the word is employed for lovers' separations or estrangements; **tui** 'from you', a sort of objective genitive NLG 200.; the whole meaning = 'the pain of being parted from you'.

se in exsilium iturum – accusative and infinitive after **confirmabat**, *esse* to be supplied with **iturum**. The exile would be with Antony, on whom it would be imposed as a punishment for his insolvency.

Section 46

quo tempore – i.e. in this time of crisis. **mala** – neuter plural of the adjective as a substantive NLG 236., 'evils', 'misadventures'. **florentissimae familiae**: either genitive, or dative of advantage NLG 188.1. Curio belonged to the *gens Scribonia*, which had achieved prominence in the second century BC. He, however, was the first from its ranks to reach the consulship (76 BC). His wealth, a military triumph awarded after his victory over the Dardani in the far north of Greece (73/72 BC) and, possibly, the censorship in 61 BC made him an influential figure and supporter of the senatorial cause. **florentissimae** refers especially to reputation.

aes alienum – 'debt'. **fili** – genitive (for *filii*) NLG 25.2. **redimeret**: the indirect command after **persuasi** continues, with *ut* understood – the same applies to **prohiberet** at the end of the sentence. The younger Curio, having stood surety for Antony's debts, had in effect taken them on himself; his father, however, was in a position to refuse settlement of them (see below, on **patrio iure et potestate**). **spe** – 'promise': Cicero praises the younger Curio's eloquence in *Brutus* 280. **facultatibus** is instrumental ablative **NLG 218.** with **redimeret. familiaritate. . .congressione** are ablatives of separation **NLG 214.2.** with **prohiberet**, while **iure et potestate** are ablative of means **NLG 218**: '... that he [Curio's father] should ban him not only from friendship but even from associating with you by his father's right and authority'. (**patrio** agrees with the nearest noun.) As *pater familias*, Curio exercised total power over his son, even as far as to decide his life and death.

haec = this intervention of Cicero to help Curio. **cum. . . meminisses**, from the verb *memini*, which is perfect in form and present in sense, translates as imperfect: 'since you remembered. . .'. The argument is that Antony would never have dared to slander such a benefactor as Cicero without the persuasion of armed men round the senate-house. Cicero is referring to the ring of steel Antony had placed inside the closed doors of the Temple of Concord, where the senate had met, on 19 September 44 BC – see 'Introduction – Historical Background'. He makes repeated mention of these **gladii** (§§ 15, 19, 104 and 112 as well as here). The **maledictis** are those Antony delivered in his speech on that date.

Section 47

sed iam marks a transition to a new angle of attack. **stupra et flagitia** – another *doublet to amplify the aspersion Cicero is casting. **omittamus** – hortatory subjunctive **NLG 274.**: 'let us pass over'. **eo liberior. . . quod**: understand *es* – 'you are the more unconstrained for the fact that. . .'; **eo** is ablative of measure of difference **NLG 223. in te admisisti** as a phrase means 'you committed'. **audire** has the sense 'to hear (said of you)'. **posses** is a generic subjunctive **NLG 283.** after **quae** – 'the sort of things which you cannot hear spoken of. . .'.

videte: Cicero turns from Antony to the rest of his (putative, since the speech does not seem to have been delivered) hearers.

festinat animus – translate this first: 'My thoughts hasten. . .'.

quae peto ut. . .: The indirect command after **peto** is **attente audiatis**. **multo notiora: multo** is another ablative of measure of difference **NLG 223.** – 'much better known'.

tamen, normally second word when it stands at the beginning of a sentence, when it picks up a concessive like **quamquam** or *quamvis* ('although'), stands first word in its clause.

debet. . .: Another inversion, where the subject of **debet** is first **cognitio** and then **recordatio** – hence the singular ending. Cicero's request is partly disingenuous: it is a form of **captatio benevolentiae*, flattering the audience that they already know perfectly well about what he will narrate, while Cicero in fact has every intention of shaping his audience's *recordatio* to suit his purposes. Cicero was also, however, absent at key moments during some of the events he brings up – from Italy (June 49 to autumn 48 BC), from Rome (autumn 48 – autumn 47 BC) and from Rome shortly before this speech (7 April to 31 August 44 BC).

etsi incidamus: The subjunctive is best taken as hortatory **NLG 274.**, not after **etsi** – the latter is here adverbial, adjusting the implication of completeness in **reliquum vitae cursum** earlier: 'even so, let us cut short. . .'. **opinor** is equivalent to 'I recommend'. **media** = 'the intervening events', i.e. after his youthful antics in the 60s BC (described in §§ 44–6) but before his career during the Civil War from 49 BC onwards (§50, **accipite nunc. . .**) – the latter, the **extrema**, is where Cicero wants to concentrate (**ad haec enim. . .** two sentences ago).

Section 48

The dative **Clodio** depends on **intimus** ('close to Clodius'). P. Clodius Pulcher, the gang-leader and enemy of Cicero, had a colourful career – including, if Plutarch is to be believed (*Cicero*, 29) a period during the prosecution of Catiline (63 BC) when he and Cicero collaborated. Soon after it, however, in 61 BC, Cicero brought evidence against Clodius, who was on trial for profaning the women-only festival of the *Bona Dea* by disguising himself as a woman and making an appearance at it. Clodius was acquitted, but took his revenge: in 59 BC when, with Caesar's help, he became a member of the plebs so that the following year (58 BC) he could be elected *tribunus plebis* (one of the ten protectors of the rights of the *plebs*, voted for each year by the people's assembly or *Concilium Plebis*). Soon afterwards he used this position to secure Cicero's exile, had his henchmen burn down Cicero's house on the Palatine, turning it then into a shrine to Libertas, and attacked Pompey when the latter was favouring Cicero's return – this was then proposed in 57 BC by one of the next year's *tribuni plebis* and mobster T. Annius Milo. In 53 BC Clodius was standing for the praetorship (a senior magistracy) and Milo for the consulship of the following year. Elections were postponed because of violence and, in January 52 BC, Milo killed Clodius in an encounter between their gangs. (Cicero has already in this speech (§§ 21–2) dealt with Antony's allegation that he, Cicero, had spurred Milo on to commit the crime.) In 58 BC Antony may have joined Clodius to avenge his stepfather P. Lentulus (§ 17) or through the mediation of Curio (§§ 44–5), who had led demonstrations on Clodius's behalf. **tribunatu** – of Clodius.

qui. . . commemorat: The argument runs, 'He, the man who claims he was kind to me, was also intimately linked with my arch-enemy.' **beneficia**: After the defeat of Pompey, whom Cicero had supported, at Pharsalus in Greece (48 BC), Caesar had banned Pompeians from re-entering Italy at the same time as inviting Cicero there. Antony, as Caesar's *magister equitum* (master of the horse = deputy), could have enforced this ban but allowed Cicero through (see § 5 above). Cicero belittles this favour (§§ 59–60).

eius. . . cuius. . . both refer to Clodius. **eius omnium incendiorum fax**: 'the spark of all that man's destructive acts' [Ramsey]. Understand *erat*. Although fax and incendium are metaphorical, **incendium** is a reminder not just of the destruction of Cicero's house on the Palatine (see last note but one) but also of the burning by Clodius's followers of the shrine of the Nymphs in the Campus Martius. **domi**: locative **NLG 49.4.**, with **cuius** = 'at whose house. . .'. **quiddam molitus est**: A wickedly insinuating phrase – 'he was up to something' – referring to Antony's secret affair with Clodius's wife Fulvia, whom he later married.

quid dicam – take this as the object (an indirect question) of **intellegit**.

inde – 'then', except that Antony, according to Plutarch (*Antony* 2.7), first went to Greece to study oratory and then served on the staff of the proconsular governor of Syria, A. Gabinius, as his *praefectus equitum*. Gabinius's father had served as quaestor under Antony's grandfather, so this might have been *quid pro quo*. **iter**: understand *fecit*, and then **Alexandream** is the accusative without *ad*, regular for cities **NLG 182.1**. This form, for *Alexandriam*, was the norm in Cicero's time. The reason for this 'journey' was the restoration to the throne of Egypt of Ptolemy XII Auletes (father of Cleopatra VII, later Antony's lover). In 59 BC, he had procured Rome's recognition of his title by bribing Caesar and his circle with 6,000 talents. But his efforts to recover this vast sum from his people by extortion induced them to depose him and, in 57 BC, he arrived at Rome to seek reinstatement. After much manoeuvring, in the course of which a Sybilline oracle emerged prohibiting the restoration of Ptolemy by military means, Gabinius agreed, thanks to another bribe this time of 10,000 talents, to invade Egypt and reinstall Ptolemy. This he did in 56 BC. **contra senatus auctoritatem**: In 57 BC the senate had decreed that the consul P. Lentulus Spinther, as soon as he had finished his year of office and become governor of Cilicia, should take on the task. Gabinius was flouting this decree and Antony, as his deputy, likewise. **contra rem publicam et religiones**: The Sybilline oracle had warned of hardships that would ensue if Ptolemy were given military assistance. Ignoring this warning was 'against the (interests of) the Republic and religious scruples' [Ramsey]. The plural *religiones* because it means 'religious considerations' rather than a particular religion.

Gabinium: A. Gabinius, as consul in 58 BC, had been complicit with Clodius in Cicero's banishment from Italy. **quicum** = *quocum*, 'in whose service'. **rectissime** drips sarcasm: '... he could do anything he wanted with perfect propriety'. On his return from his governorship of Syria in 54 BC, Gabinius was charged with *maiestas* (treason against the state), *res repetundae* (extortion) and *ambitus* (bribery). Cicero was persuaded by Pompey to defend him, but was probably not sorry to see him condemned under the second accusation. Antony had every reason to distance himself from Rome and from guilt by contagion.

qui... reditus: qui is an adjective, with **reditus**. **aut qualis** might be translated, 'or should I say under what circumstances?' See previous note for Gabinius's record.

prius... domum: Understand *iit*. **domum** does not require *ad* **NLG 182.1**. Take **prius** with **quam**, as commonly **NLG 291**. **ultimam... Galliam**: Caesar, who seems to have been legate to Antony's father M. Antonius Creticus, welcomed Antony to his campaign in northern

Gaul, where he had been forced by tribal insurrection to overwinter. There, as well as avoiding Rome, the ambitious Antony could seek further military distinction.

quae autem domus? Understand *ei erat*. In §62, Antony's acquisition is mentioned of a house which had belonged to L. Piso – but this was in 48 BC.

suam... quisque: A frequent collocation **NLG 244.4**. 'each... his own'. **tum** – at a time before the Civil Wars disrupted ownership through the seizure and auctioning of property.

quid erat... tenebas?: in tuo, understand *fundo* (farm). **poneres** is subjunctive of purpose after **ubi NLG 282.2**: 'What (place) on earth was there where you might set foot on your own land...' **Misenum** is an adjective, 'at Misenum' (again with *fundum* understood). Misenum is a promontory on the bay of Naples, a naval base. Antony's paternal grandfather had bequeathed him this property, but it too was mortgaged to his debts, as **cum sociis** indicates. **Sisaponem**: Sisapo was a town in the province of Hispania Ulterior where mining took place for cinnabar – a mercury compound much valued as a bright red pigment. The mines were worked by corporations, much as Antony's rural villa was shared with other co-owners.

Section 49

venis – historic present (used in narrative as a vivid equivalent of a perfect **NLG 259.3.**). This almost as natural here in English as in Latin. **ad quaesturam petendam**: Antony returned from Gaul in late 53 BC to stand for the quaestorship of 52 BC at the same time as Clodius was campaigning for election to the praetorship (see previous chapter, on P. Clodius Pulcher). Antony was starting to climb the succession of positions that led to the highest office, the so-called *cursus honorum* – in Republican times this comprised:

- quaestorship
- (aedileship OR tribunate of the people i.e. *tribunus plebis*)
- praetorship
- consulship
- censorship

Holders of these offices were members of the senate and remained so when their term finished.

aude dicere: Much like 'I dare you to make out that...'. **parentem**: Antony's mother, Julia Antonia – daughter of L. Caesar (consul of 90 BC) and a distant cousin of Julius Caesar. (Antony's father, M. Antonius Creticus, had died after his defeat by the pirates off Crete in 72–1 BC; see also note on §44). **prius**: Take with the **quam** that follows (as in §48).

ut... a te: The phrase **acceperam... litteras** implies a request – 'I had... received a letter... (asking) that...'. **satis fieri**: As an intransitive verb taking the dative, the passive of **satisfacio** must be impersonal **NLG 187.II.b**. Literally '... I should allow amends to be made by you to me'. These amends are for the damage Antony did to Cicero as an ally of Clodius (§48; **tuis in me iniuriis** later in this chapter). Cicero seems to imply that, when Antony physically attacked Clodius (as soon to be narrated), it was with encouragement from Caesar; Clodius had fallen out with him after Caesar had supported the bill proposing Cicero's return from exile. **itaque**: The standard word order would be *te de gratia ne loqui quidem passus sum*. **ne loqui quidem... gratia**: A service rendered could imply an obligation in return; Cicero is at pains to repudiate any hint that he placed Antony under such an obligation (hence the word order, with **ne... quidem** to stress **loqui** at the start and **gratia** dismissed at the end). **gratia** – the favour of overlooking Clodius's offences.

observatus: 'shown honour to'. This represents a measure of support, if not whole-hearted.

es conatus occidere – more normally *occidere conatus es*. Cicero has already brought up this incident (§21). After Milo had killed Clodius (see note to §48), Antony joined in his prosecution; although Cicero defended him (with two other advocates), the outcome was Milo's conviction. **cumque... tamen: cum** here 'although' **NLG 309.3.**, as the **tamen** first word indicates (see note on §47). **ita praedicabas: ita** introduces a double indirect statement in which **te** does duty first as the subject of **existimare** and then as the subject of **esse facturum**. **nisi... interfecisses**: The pluperfect subjunctive because the verb in the protasis, which would have been future perfect in direct speech, is now in *oratio obliqua* **NLG 319.**

in quo – 'As a result of this...' **demiror** is stronger than *miror* – 'My jaw drops at the idea that...' **rem illam... idem illud** both refer to the assassination of Clodius. Also in §21, Cicero had rejected the allegation that he had anything to do with Milo's crime; he admits he approved of Clodius's removal, but distinguishes that from instigating it. **cum** = 'since'. **te... deferentem**: 'When you were of your own accord delivering that same service for me'. Cicero argues that, as with Antony so with Milo, in neither case did he egg them on.

quamquam – 'and yet', as a conjunction at the start of the sentence **NLG 309.5. perseverares**: This is subjunctive for an unreal conditional, and imperfect because the future act is viewed in past time: 'if you were going to persevere in this'. **malebam**: Indicative **NLG 304.3. rem illam** – once again, the assassination of Clodius is meant. **ad tuam gloriam** is in *antithesis to **ad meam gratiam** – two trisyllables with 'g' *alliteration.

Section 50

quaestor es factus: 'You were elected quaestor'. Apparently, though campaigning in 53 BC, Antony held the quaestorship in 51BC. Thus he would have been elected in 52 BC, a year after returning to Rome; this makes the reasons Cicero gives for Antony's departure from Rome in the next sentence less plausible. His haste to Caesar (**ad Caesarem cucurristi**) may well have been due to the rebellion of Vercingetorix in 52 BC; before the end of that year, Antony was in attendance at the siege of Alesia (Caesar, *Bello Gallico*, 7.81.6). **continuo** means 'directly (after the election)'. Quaestors were assigned their tours of duty by lot (**sorte**) – or could be appointed to one by decree of the senate (**senatus consulto** – more precisely, an **extra sortem senatus consultum**). What may well have happened in Antony's case is that he departed before the decree of the senate was ratified, simply because Caesar needed him urgently. In that case Cicero is telling the literal truth but implying a breach of procedure which did not in fact exist. **sine lege**: 'Without legal warrant' – not required unless Antony had broken the normal procedure, and this is only Cicero's implication.

id enim. . . ducebas: unum goes with **perfugium**, 'sole refuge from. . .'. **in terris** – 'in the world'. **duco** is commonly used to mean 'I consider'. The genitives **egestatis, aeris alieni, nequitiae**, all depend on **perfugium. perditis. . . rationibus** is an ablative absolute **NLG 227.**, 'When you had squandered your means of livelihood' (Lacey). **ratio**, 'manner' or 'method', is regularly in the plural. In §78 Caesar is described as recruiting from the ranks of the indebted where he detected in them suitable recklessness.

ibi te. . .: te is the object of **explevisses. hoc** looks forward to the infinitive **expilare** – a conjecture to fill a gap in the text; it has plausibility because a scribe might readily conflate it with **explere**

(so-called 'haplography'). **effundas** is best taken as a (sarcastic) subjunctive of purpose **NLG 282.2**. – 'If this is glutting oneself, to plunder something immediately to spill it out'. **advolasti** for *advolavisti* **NLG 116.1**. – 'flew for protection', as explained by **egens**: once appointed to a magistracy, Antony could be pursued by his creditors. **tribunatum**: Antony was elected *tibunus plebis* for 49 BC and entered office, as normal, in December the previous year. **viri tui**: Genitive with **similis**. *vir* is a pejorative word for a homosexual lover – 'husband', pronounced with a sneer (*vir* was also used to epitomise manly qualities). Curio had been *tribunus plebis* in 50 BC; Caesar had purchased his support with a considerable bribe. Cicero obviously did not need to spell out the resemblance.

Confirmatio 44–114 continues:

Partitio 50b: Now please listen to the damage he inflicted on the whole Republic [his tribunate].

Sections 51–55a: When the senate, in 49 BC, wished to shore up the Republic [by requiring Caesar to surrender his army in Gaul] and, as far as possible, respect Caesar's interests, you, Antony [as tribune of the people], blocked it from doing so – it had no option but to pass the *senatus consultum ultimum* [a decree of emergency powers, in effect martial law, which would have allowed the senate to act against Antony and Cassius]. If you had not fled to Caesar's forces, you would not have escaped retribution. Caesar then was able to march on Rome under the pretext that he was defending the trampled rights of Antony as tribune. The senior magistrates quitted Italy and war followed, the blame for which must be laid at your, Antony's, door.

Sections 55b–58: Antony's restoration of rights in 49 BC to certain condemned men during Caesar's absence from Italy did not include his own uncle. On the other hand he did pardon L. Denticulus, a gambling friend, probably in repayment of his gaming losses. Then, on a tour of Italy, he travelled in a carriage with his mistress, the actress Cytheris, and awarded himself lictors wearing laurel crowns [absurd pomp to which he was not entitled].

Sections 59–63: Antony, as one of Caesar's right-hand men [at Pharsalus, the battle at which Pompey was defeated, he commanded the left flank], participated in the blood-letting of 48 BC. Then, at Brundisium, he did not harm Cicero [see §§ 5 – 7a above]. Then you met up with Cytheris and resumed your tour of Italy. Appointed *magister equitum* [master of the horse, deputy], you appropriated M. Piso's house and enriched yourself with inheritances stolen from the legitimate heirs. Most disgusting of all, this master of the horse, the day after a wedding feast, before a gathering of the Roman people, filled his lap and the platform with his vomit.

Sections 64–70: When Caesar, in 47 BC, returned from Alexandria to Rome, he put Pompey's confiscated property up for auction – Antony, the sole bidder, acquired Pompey's entire estate, and with it the opprobrium of the community. He set about squandering the whole estate. And now he claims virtue himself because he divorced Cytheris. He refers to himself as 'both consul and Antony', unaware that he draws attention by this to his shamelessness.

Sections 71–74: Then it came to paying for the purchase of Pompey's estate. Caesar, returned from his African campaign in 46 BC, pressed Antony for what he owed; Antony at first refused on the grounds that what he had gained was his rightful share of the booty. Caesar sent soldiers to demand cash. Antony attempted to re-auction what was left – but was prevented by the heirs to one of the estates Antony had illegitimately obtained. In despair, Antony is said to have sent the assassin who was detected in Caesar's house. Caesar left the following day for Spain, having granted Antony an extension.

Sections 75–78a: In the campaign against Pompey's sons in Spain [Gnaeus and Sextus Pompeius had taken command of the remaining Pompeian forces there], you took no part – you set off but say you could not reach the country safely. Dolabella [P. Cornelius Dolabella, Cicero's son-in-law, a notorious dissolute and opponent of Antony], by contrast, fought in all three of Caesar's major battles against his fellow-citizens [Pharsalus, Thapsus, Munda], even though, unlike you, he had not become the owner of Pompey's property – and it was for this, in part, that Pompey's sons were fighting. Instead you stopped at Narbo, in Gaul, and campaigned for the consulship. You returned to Rome and, disguised as a messenger, to your wife [Fulvia, whom Cicero studiously does not mention by name]; you delivered a letter saying Antony had given up his mistress, then revealed yourself. But the real reason for your return was to halt foreclosure on the guarantors of your debts.

Section 78

C. Caesari: After taking some seven months to subdue the last Pompeian forces, Caesar returned to Italy in about June 45 BC. The dative depends on **obviam**, 'to meet...'. **longissime** – as far as Narbo again, where Caesar broke his return journey to Italy.

isti, redisti: Abbreviated forms **NLG 116.1.** of *iisti, rediisti* – *asyndeton for the breathless shuttling, but the expression seems to have been colloquial, cf. 'came and went'. Narbo – Rome – Narbo is probably what Cicero means. **si minus NLG 306.2.** = 'if not', typically where a verb (here **cognosceret**) is shared across clauses.

factus es ei...: **ei** goes with **familiaris**. We are told by Plutarch (*Antony* 11.1) that, on his jouney back from Spain through Italy, Caesar made Antony his fellow passenger in his carriage while D. Brutus and C. Octavius (his main heir, the future Augustus) were carried along behind. **rursus** because of the interval since the Pharsalian campaign. **nescio quo modo**: 'somehow or other' – deliberately disparaging. For **nescio quis** as a compound adjective (or pronoun), see **NLG 254.6.**

habebat hoc...: Understand **hoc** *(moris)*, 'this way of behaving'. **omnino** – 'absolutely', i.e. without exception.

quem plane...recipiebat: The antecedent is absorbed into the relative clause **NLG 251.4.**, '<him> whom he (had) discovered (to be) ...' – and is picked up again at **hunc. cognorat**, the abbreviated form of **cognoverat NLG 116.1.**, does double duty, for the relative as well as the conditional clause. The pluperfect indicative implies repeated action in the past **NLG 302.3.** – 'who(ever)..., if (ever). Be careful with the conjunctions – **perditum...egentemque, nequam... audacemque**. Also **nequam** is an indeclinable adjective.

Section 79

his... rebus: i.e. by all the apparent drawbacks of character and situation. **praeclare commendatus** is sarcastic: 'resoundingly recommended (for these virtues)'. *commendatio* is the term for publicly supporting a candidate for office; **renuntiari** – 'be officially proclaimed'; **renuntio** is the term for returning the result of an election. Cicero, however, by **iussus es**, is showing a different mechanism at work – Caesar's influence (but see style note). **consul... et quidem cum ipso**: i.e. Antony and Caesar were together to be the consuls for 44 BC.

nihil queror de Dolabella: 'I make no complaint about (the treatment of) Dolabella'. P. Cornelius Dolabella, mentioned in § 75, first sided with Pompey in the civil wars but changed into one of Caesar's loyal lieutenants, as a commander of a fleet in the Adriatic and then as a senior officer at the battles of Pharsalus, Thapsus and Munda. He became Cicero's son-in-law in 50 and *tribunus plebis* in 47; associated himself with Caesar's assassins in 44 and became consul; finally, through Antony's mediation, he was appointed governor of Syria, where he killed the pro-consul, was declared a public enemy and committed suicide (43). Cicero's aim here is to portray Antony's behaviour as even worse than Caesar's, whom Cicero pretends Antony manipulated for his own purposes. Cicero's story is that Caesar promised the full consulship of 44 BC to Dolabella, as a reward for his service in Spain and Africa, but then, persuaded by Antony (Dolabella's enemy), broke that promise and took the consulship on himself. This is unlikely: Caesar had been consul in 46 and 45 BC, so would probably have intended to hold the post again in 44 BC until he departed, in the March of his death, on his proposed campaign of Parthia (the thorn in the Roman empire's eastern side). He would have had time to order affairs before handing them over to a replacement (suffect) consul. The suffect, who never gave his name to the year, was in a less honourable position, more appropriate to Dolabella who had not risen through the *cursus honorum* (see note above on §49), but only been *tribunus plebis* in 47 BC. Besides, Caesar, who would have known of the antipathy between Antony and Dolabella, would scarcely have planned to set them on an equal footing. Antony would have expressed opposition to Dolabella's suffect consulship in 45 BC, been unsuccessful and then taken the steps described over the next chapters in 44 BC to block Dolabella's election as suffect consul.

quanta... perfidia: Ablative of description or quality **NLG 224**. This allows Cicero to pick the word **perfidia** up again in the next sentence which, if he had used *perfidiosus*, he could not have done so plainly. **uterque vestrum** – 'each of the two of you', **vestrum** being genitive plural of *vos* **NLG 84**.

quis ignorat: Take first – i.e. *quis ignorat quanta perfidia...*, 'Who is unaware how treacherous...'

ille induxit...: **ille** is Caesar; understand *eum* (Dolabella) as the object of **induxit. promissum et receptum** – 'what was promised and accepted'; understand *consulatum*. **intervertit ad seque transtulit: ad se** is treated as one word for the addition of **–que**. Cicero leaves it vague how Caesar did this, indeed could have done this – but that is consistent with his treatment of Caesar as absolute monarch (**regem**, §80). **tu... ascripsisti: perfidiae** is dative after **ascribo; eius** refers to Caesar. 'You put the responsibility for what was your own desire on Caesar's perfidy', i.e. Caesar did what you wanted (the implication is that Antony asked him) and so you could, and did, blame him for betraying Dolabella.

veniunt and **cogimur** are historic presents **NLG 259.3**. Cicero provides a little narrative vignette of the senate's meeting. There is no hint of compulsion in **cogimur** – 'assembled'. **Kalendae Ianuariae**:

The inaugural gathering of the senate under the year's new consuls took place on 1 January.

invectus... ego: The word order is deliberately ungainly, to suit an uncomfortable occasion – *Dolabella in istum multo copiosius et paratius quam nunc ego invectus est*. **in istum**: against Antony. Under Cicero's account, Dolabella was well aware that Antony was responsible for his being cheated of the consulship proper. In fact (see previous note) Dolabella might earlier have had reasons for inveighing against Antony, if the latter had spoken against his suffect consulship. **paratius** – comparative of *paratus*, 'with greater preparation', 'more calculatedly'; Cicero is being disingenuous.

Section 80

hic autem: **hic** refers to Antony. **quae** is exclamatory; **di** is the vocative plural of *deus* **NLG 25.4**. The speech of Antony's referred to is that in response to Dolabella in the senate on 1 January 44 BC.

primum cum...: This **cum** clause is interrupted by the parenthesis **quem negant... diceret** and is reprised by **sed cum Caesar ita dixisset, tum....** It translates naturally enough. **prius quam proficisceretur** – for Parthia (see note in previous chapter), to which Caesar planned in 44 BC to go for up to three years; Crassus's humiliating defeat by the Parthians at Carrhae took place in 53 BC. The moment when Caesar unveiled his plan to leave Dolabella as consul is likely to have been in 45 BC; see note on §79, **nihil queror de Dolabella. se...Dolabellam consulem esse iussurum**: 'that he would order that Dolabella be consul' – a second *esse* is understood after **iussurum**. After **primum**, one might expect *deinde* or similar, but Cicero allows himself, in the next chapter, to be carried away by Antony's silly mismanagement of his own cause.

quem negant ... diceret: quem is equivalent to *et eum*, eum being Caesar – *et eum negant regem (esse)*, 'and they say he isn't a despot, when he...'. **regem** is loaded with the odium Romans reserved for the last of their kings, L. Tarquinius Superbus, expelled from Rome in 510/509 BC, whose kingship was superseded by the Republic – see § 87, where Cicero mentions him by name. **qui...faceret...diceret**: These are generic subjunctives, with a concessive implication **NLG 283.3.b.** – literally, 'although he was of such a kind as to'. **faceret semper eius modi aliquid**: For *aliquid eius modi semper faceret*.

ita dixisset: This resumes the earlier **cum** clause, 'but when Caesar had spoken in this way'. **bonus** is ironical – as Cicero's lengthy commentary on Antony's incompetence soon makes obvious. **augur**: The augurs, who at this time formed a *collegium* with sixteen members, had the responsibility to discover by observing signs (*auguria*), either casually met with (*oblativa*) or watched for (*impetrativa*), whether the gods approved or disapproved of a proposed action. These signs were often to do with the flight of birds (hence the speculative etymology of *augur* from *avis*, 'bird') – but could also be phenomena like a clap of thunder or an earth tremor. Cicero in this and the next chapter uses very specific terminology: when an augur announced an omen (*nuntiatio*), if that omen was unfavourable, the proposed action was automatically abandoned. An augur could not, however, declare that he would look for omens (*spectio*); this was a privilege reserved for magistrates, above all consuls, who (under the law mentioned in the next chapter – see note on **per leges**) had to make any unfavourable announcement (*obnuntiatio*) in person and in advance of the proposed action. No proof was demanded of *auguria* that a magistrate, or an augur, had detected – so this was a powerful method of obstruction. **eo** goes with **sacerdotio** (the augurship), itself governed by **praeditum**. Thus, augurship of Antony's has already been mentioned in §4. **impedire...vitiare**: By announcing *auguria* *oblativa* which were unfavourable, Antony could block (**impedire**) the elections before they happened or render them void (**vitiare**) if they had already been completed.

in quo... cognoscite: Take **cognoscite** after **in quo. primum** picks up the same word at the start of the chapter. **hominis** – refers to Antony, with condescension or scorn (see style note on §78, **familiaris**).

Section 81

quid enim? 'For why is that?' A *rhetorical question which introduces – and at the same time postpones – the explanation of **incredibilem stupiditatem. istud**- i.e. the blocking of the elections. **sacerdoti** for *sacerdotii* **NLG 25.2**. – Cicero is referring to Anthony's augurship again. **si augur non esses et consul esses**: The argument here is that Antony could have achieved what he was trying to do as a consul just as, or better than, as an augur: Antony is consul, but the conditional implies that he is scarcely a proper one. 'If you weren't being augur and were being consul....'.

vide ne etiam facilius: ne is used here on the analogy of a fear clause ., for an (ironically) cautious assertion – 'See if it might be the case that...'. **facilius** – understand *facere potuisses*.

nos because Cicero was also an augur.

esto: Future imperative of sum **NLG 100.**, used to mean 'so be it' – granting something before moving on (to **sed impudentia**). **hoc imperite: imperite** is the adverb of *imperitus*; understand *dixit*. **ab homine** goes with **postulanda**, with *sunt* understood – 'are to be expected of a man....'. **numquam sobrio** – 'never sober', cf §63, Antony the drunkard, or §84.

multis ante mensibus: 'Many months before', **ante** as an adverb used with the ablative of measure of difference **NLG 223, 357.1**. If Cicero is referring to threats Antony made in the senate on 1 January, since the suffect consul elections seem to have taken place in early March at the latest, he is palpably exaggerating. It makes more sense to interpret this as referring to Antony's opposition to Dolabella expressed the previous year (see note to §79, **nihil queror de Dolabella**). **Dolabellae comitia**: The elections for the suffect consul in 44 BC. **aut prohibiturum auspiciis aut id facturum esse quod fecit: aut... aut...** give the only two possibilities, as Antony wishes the senate to grasp what he would make inevitable (cf. **vel...vel...** for exactly the same threat at the end of §80; **vel impedire vel vitiare**, but there Antony was suggesting what he could do, here he is declaring what he will do). **id facturum quod fecit** is amplified in §83, where it becomes clear that Antony did not prevent the electoral assembly from meeting (**impedire, prohibiturum**) but declared its proceedings void through unfavourable auspices (**vitiare**).

quisquamne... constituit?: The point here is that the only person who could claim to foresee what future auspices would hold was someone who decided to look out for them. This was precisely the *spectio* (see note on **ita dixisset**, §80) reserved for magistrates other than augurs, and Antony was speaking on 1 January as an augur. If a magistrate did announce a *spectio*, a meeting would be suspended until he declared that he had, or had not, witnessed unfavourable auspices. **quid viti** for *quid vitii* (for genitive form see **NLG 25.2.**; for partitive genitive after **quid**, see **NLG 201.2.**); 'what flaw', introducing an indirect question. **nisi qui** = 'except (a person) who...'. **de caelo servare**: A technical phrase for 'observe an omen' (cf. *de Divinatione*, ii.74)

quod neque licet comitiis per leges: This sentence is built around **neque... et... NLG 341.3**. The connecting **quod** (object of **nuntiare**, at the end of the sentence), means something inauspicious (**quid**

viti); **comitiis** is ablative of time when **NLG 230.1.**: you cannot, under the laws (**per leges**) make your *obnuntiatio* (announcement of unfavourable auspices) while the elections are going on; you must do so, as Cicero goes on to say, before they have started. He seems to be invoking a law passed by P. Clodius in 58 BC, which stipulated just this, apparently in a bid to deter excessive obstruction through auspices. Thus Antony, as an augur, was entitled to declare proceedings invalid while they were happening (which is what he did – see §83), but not to predict that he will do so. **non comitiis habitis**: The context requires that **habitis** does duty for the non-existent present passive participle, 'not once the elections are being held'.

verum implicata inscientia impudentia est: **impudentia** is nominative (picking up from the same word earlier in this chapter), **inscientiā** ablative.

nec scit. . .: This needs filling out – **nec scit quod augurem** [sc. *scire decet*] **nec facit quod pudentem** [sc. *facere*] **decet**.

Section 82

ex illo die. . . usque ad Idus Martias: 'From than day right up to the Ides of March' (and Caesar's assassination). Cicero turns to Antony's consulship.

quis. . . apparitor?: **quis** as an adjective **NLG 90.2.b**.; understand *fuit*. An **apparitor** was attendant on a Roman magistrate, such as a lictor, clerk or *praeco* (herald).

nihil ipse poterat: **nihil** is an internal accusative/accusative of result **NLG 176.2.b**. – 'He could (do) nothing'. Given that Antony promptly proceeds to obstruct Dolabella's election, which was not Caesar's wish, the tone here must be highly ironical.

caput... petebat: Cicero paints the absurd picture of Antony trailing behind Caesar's litter like an attendant, poking his head in the curtains at the rear to consult his fellow consul (**conlega**). Although litters were normally used by women and invalids, they could offer an opportunity for extra work (cf. Pliny the Elder, in Pliny *Letters*, iii.5.15). Caesar's health was also by now more fragile – but that seems inadequate to explain his regularly travelling by litter. **beneficia quae venderet**: Subjunctive of purpose in the relative clause **NLG 282.2**.

ecce Dolabellae comitiorum dies – in late February or early March. **Dolabellae** because he appears to have been the only candidate for suffect consul.

sortitio praerogativae: sc. *fit*. 'The choice was made by lot of the century to vote first'. The assembly responsible for electing consuls and praetors, the *comitia centuriata*, voted in order of census class (i.e. based on degree of wealth), the result of each vote being declared before the next one was taken. As soon as a majority had been reached out of the 193 centuries in total (i.e. 97 for one candidate), the election was over. The order of voting, insofar as it can be pieced together from the main evidence (Livy i.43; Dio Cassius; Cicero *Republic* 2.39), was as follows:

- *prima classis* – 35 centuries of *iuniores*, men of military age (18 – 46); 35 centuries of *seniores* (47 and above); 12 centuries of *equites*; 1 century of artisans
- *suffragia* – the 6 centuries of equites which constituted the original cavalry force under the kings (added to the preceding *prima classis* = 89 centuries)
- *secunda classis* (of 22 centuries), *tertia* (of 20 centuries), *quarta* (of 22 centuries), *quinta* (of 40 centuries), making the 104 remaining centuries, each with subdivisions into *seniores* and *iuniores* – though there is uncertainty about the precise constitution of these classes and the numbers of centuries in them; Dio Cassius even has a sixth class.

To start proceedings, one century of the *iuniores* in the *prima classis* was drawn by lot, the *centuria praerogativa*. This voted first; its verdict was announced (**renuntiatur**) and was regarded as a strong influence on the subsequent voting of the other centuries. **quiescit**: i.e. Antony – historic present **NLG 259.3.**, as are the remaining verbs in the chapter. If Antony had seen that the outcome was going Dolabella's way – as Cicero implies he could – then it would have made sense for him to interrupt the process earlier than he did.

renuntiatur: 'The result was announced', by implication in favour of Dolabella.

prima classis vocatur: The rest of the first class, after the *centuria praerogativa* had gone ahead. **deinde. . . suffragia**: The 6 centuries of cavalry who voted before the *secunda classis*. sc. *vocantur*. **ita ut adsolet**: sc. *fieri*, 'as usually happens'.

quae omnia. . . dixi: 'All of which was done. . .' – a pardonable *hyperbole to move from the protracted voting to Antony's delayed intervention.

Section 83

confecto negotio: 'When the business was over', i.e. once a majority had been reached in Dolabella's favour. If Dolabella was indeed the only candidate, this would not have been far into the *secunda classis* (see note on previous chapter) – of the centuries which voted before it, the *prima classis* provided 83 out of the 97 required for a majority, the *suffragia* another 6. **bonus** – sarcastic in the extreme. **C. Laelium**: Laelius, consul in 140 BC, was an augur and bore the cognomen '*Sapiens*' (hence Cicero's barbed allusion to him here). He was friends with Scipio Africanus Minor (the adoptive grandson of Scipio Africanus) and is the main spokesman in Cicero's philosophical dialogue *de Amicitia*, roughly contemporary with this speech. **diceres** – 'you might pronounce him' **'alio die'**: These are the words of an *obnuntiatio*, the declaration of an unfavourable omen, and would cause a meeting to be adjourned and/or voided its actions.

de caelo servasse: For …*servavisse* **NLG 116. neque… dixisti… nec… dicis**: If Antony had said this, it would have been as part of a *spectio* (see §81 note).

id igitur… praedixeras: Cicero is recalling what Antony had said in his attack on Dolabella at the inaugural senate for the consuls on 1 January (§79) – and his own condemnation of predicting future omens (§81). **tanto ante praedixeras**: Either Antony had claimed this on 1 January or had done so on a separate occasion – most likely when Caesar proposed Dolabella as suffect in the previous year (see note on §79).

magna… calamitate: Ablative of attendant circumstance **NLG 221**. – 'to your, rather than the Republic's, great detriment'. **obstrinxisti** – 'you hamstrung'. Even a fraudulent omen could not be disregarded – in *de Divinatione* (i.29) Cicero recounts how Crassus marched to his death (see note to §80) even when the auspices had been condemned as fake. **augur auguri, consul consuli**: Caesar was the augur opposed – although as *pontifex maximus* he should not have held the position, he had himself appointed in 47 BC and featured the augur's wand (*lituus*) on his coins. The consul opposed could be either Caesar (in office) or more likely Dolabella (just elected). **obnuntiasti** – for *obnuntiavisti* **NLG 7.2**.

nolo plura – sc. *dicere*. **ne acta… convellere**: Any legislation passed by Antony with Dolabella was vulnerable if Dolabella's election was invalid – this point is scored against Antony by Cicero in *Philippic*

3.9 and 5.9, where he of course does not mention that Antony later accepted Dolabella as consul (§84). On **acta**, see note on § 100, **acta enim Caesaris**.

ad nostrum conlegium: i.e. the college of augurs. It does not seem that the arbitration ever took place.

Section 84

quam diu tu voles... creatus: The future indicative of **voles** is suitably acid – Antony (cf. **provideras... praedixeras...**) in the last chapter determines what will happen. Translate, however, as present – 'As long as you wish...'. **vitiosus** = 'invalidly elected'; **salvis auspiciis** is ablative of manner NLG 218. /instrument NLG 220. Antony recognised Dolabella as suffect consul at a meeting of the senate on 17 March 44 BC – Dolabella had taken up office and aligned himself with the Liberators (Caesar's assassins), so Antony became conciliatory.

si nihil est... requiro: Cicero's argument is that either Antony did not mean the words **'alio die'**, or he realised their force but was not uttering them as an augur should. We are, in other words, returned to the cleft stick of **impudentia** (irresponsibility) – **imprudentia** (negligence). **nuntiasti** for *nuntiavisti* NLG 7.2. **confitere** is imperative. **sobrium non fuisse**: Antony the drunkard, as §81 and note. **ea quae sit**: 'What that (force) is', referring to *vis*. **augur** = 'as augur'.

sed ne forte...: Here follows a digression from the theme of auspices, resumed in §88. The next section concerns the **Lupercalia**, a festival that took place on 15 February – Cicero is preserving chronological order. The Luperci were the priests of Lycean Pan, who protected flocks from wolves. To celebrate him, the Luperci, of whom Antony was one, sacrificed goats and a dog at the cave of the Lupercal, below the Palatine hill, in which Romulus and Remus had been suckled by a she-wolf. The Luperci then ran around the hill wearing only a goat-skin about their waists and struck those they encountered, particularly women, with thongs of goat-hide. These blows were apparently purificatory and symbolised the promotion of fertility. **unam** – 'one particular (deed)', in contrast with **multis. pulcherrimam** is again sarcastic. **veniamus** is hortatory subjunctive **NLG 274.**, 'let us move on'.

non dissimulat: Cicero keeps up the pretence that the speech was delivered in Antony's presence. **apparet** *(sc. eum)* **esse commotum**: 'It appears that he is perturbed'.

quidlibet... fecit: The text is doubtful here, and it is possible that a marginal gloss (explanation) has intruded. If we take **faciat** as jussive **NLG 275.** and the word order as *quidlibet faciat, modo ne nauseet, quod...*, the sense is reasonably clear: 'Let him do whatever he pleases, provided he doesn't spew up, as (**quod**) he did in the portico of Minucius' (a building on the Campus Martius, where Antony was at the time dealing with public business). Cicero has already told this anecdote in §63 (see style note to §50), in repellent detail. **modo ne** ('provided that... not'), see **NLG 310.II.**

cupio audire...: Cicero challenges Antony to produce an adequate defence, implying that his eloquence is insufficient even after he had employed a coach in rhetoric, Sex. Clodius, and rewarded him with a large grant of land (**campus**) near Leontini, in Sicily (as described in § 43). **ubi rhetoris sit tanta merces** = 'where such an enormous fee to your instructor has gone'.

Section 85

in rostris: The speaker's platform, moved by Julius Caesar from the south of the senate house to the western end of the forum and hence known as the Rostra Nova, was ornamented with the prows of ships (*rostra*) captured at the battle of Antium (338 BC, between Rome and the Volsci). **conlega tuus** – Caesar. **toga purpurea... coronatus**: It seems that the purple toga, a symbol of royalty, was distinct from the *vestis triumphalis*, also purple but richly embroidered with golden stars, which Caesar had been voted by the senate the previous year. This toga, the *sella aurea* and the crown – a version of that worn by a triumphal general – were recent honours, again voted by the senate. Dio Cassius says that the crown Caesar wore at the Lupercalia was gilded. He could hardly have made a more kingly impression.

ita eras Lupercus... deberes: Literally 'you were a priest of the Luperci in such a way that you should have remembered...', i.e. 'although you were a priest of the Luperci, you should have remembered...' (concessive). A third college of Luperci had been added, also in Caesar's honour, to the previous two; these were known as the Julian Luperci, and Antony was their *magister*. Cicero is referring to the nakedness of the priests at this festival (see note on previous chapter, *Lupercalia*). In *Philippic* 3.12, Cicero says by his conduct here he abdicated from consular office.

diadema: 'A diadem was a headband made of a flat strip of white cloth knotted behind and having the ends dangling' [Ramsey]. Alexander the Great had adopted it as a symbol of monarchy – clearly the bestowal of it on Caesar at a public festival amounted to popular acceptance of him as king (not merely another honour).

gemitus sc. *sunt*. **unde...?** sc. *adeptus es*.

abiectum: 'lying discarded', sc *diadema*. The tribunes Flavus and Marcellus had only weeks earlier removed a diadem from a statue of Caesar; this could be what Cicero is referring to here. **meditatum et cogitatum scelus**: Accusative in apposition to the sentence', i.e. to what has preceded: 'a deliberate and considered crime'. Scholarly opinion differs on what was in fact going on here – but it seems unlikely that Antony would have attempted to surprise Caesar with such an impromptu presentation, whether he intended it to confirm Caesar's power or to embarrass him. More probable is that Caesar had arranged this curious charade with Antony so that he could be seen refusing a public confirmation of his status – but this too is not straightforward, since the attire Caesar had chosen to wear was thoroughly royal. It may be that Caesar wished to show that he accepted honours voted by the senate, but would not allow himself to receive the equivalent from the people.

imponebas, sc. *Caesari*... **reiciebat**: The imperfects matter – 'you were trying to put on... he kept on rejecting (it)'. The first is conative **NLG 260.3**, the second iterative **NLG 260.2**.

inventus es qui... idem...: The **idem** picks up the **qui** after the long **cum** clause has intervened; translate as e.g. 'you, indeed...'. **auctor regni** – 'founder of a monarchy', 'king-maker'. **conlegam... dominum** – 'as fellow-consul... as master', both in apposition to **quem. temptares** – generic subjunctive **NLG 283.**, '(who) would test'.

Section 86

at etiam... captabas: etiam = 'even', **captabas** is conative imperfect **NLG 260.3** ('you were trying to win...'). **supplex**: Making oneself a suppliant (**supplex**) to a victor was a commonplace of epic battle, but here a different form of self-abasement is meant: *proskynesis*, the custom under the Persian kings and the Hellenistic monarchs who came after them, which should therefore have been anathema to a free-spirited Roman.

quid petens? ut servires?: ut depends on **petens NLG 296**. 'Seeking what? To be a slave?'

peteres: potential subjuntive – 'you might seek (this, i.e. to be a slave). . .; you certainly weren't acting on the people's authority.' **omnia paterere: paterere** is the alternative form of *patereris*. Cicero is referring to the excesses of Antony already detailed in § 44. **ut facile servires**: a second purpose in parallel with **ut omnia paterere. facile** means here 'readily', 'naturally'.

a nobis populoque Romano mandatum: Cicero is anticipating the start of the next chapter, where he mentions that a note was added in the Fasti (the Roman calendar, displayed publicly), saying that Antony on this day had handed over kingship to Caesar. Here he says denies that Antony had any mandate to do so from the powers that mattered, the senate (**nobis**) and people. **id certe: id** refers to offering Caesar the crown; **certe** 'at any rate'.

o praeclaram. . . eloquentiam: Accusative of exclamation **NLG 183**. Antony's eloquence has already been skewered (end of § 84); here the ridiculousness is more the incongruity of his (lack of) dress and what he attempts to do – **contionatus** is deliberately chosen because a *contio* is an assembly called by a magistate or priest; Antony had the right to call one as a consul, but as such should have been wearing his *toga praetexta*, not a loin-cloth (**nudus** – see note Lupercalia on § 84). **cum es. . . contionatus: cum** meaning 'at the time when' takes the indicative **NLG 288.1**.

quid. . . dignius?: Supply *sit*.

num exspectas dum... fodiamus?: dum with subjunctive = 'until', where the event is anticipated **NLG 293.III.2** – it is normal after **exspecto**: 'Surely you weren't waiting for us to...?' **stimulis**: goads were commonly used for punishing slaves, and even more commonly for coercing goats.

haec te... oratio: The word order is deliberately anguished – *Haec oratio, si ullam partem sensus habes, te lacerat, haec (oratio te) cruentat*. **partem sensus** – 'scrap of feeling'.

vereor... commotus: imminuam is subjunctive in the fear clause **NLG 296.2, dicam** future indicative. **summorum virorum** – refers to Caesar's assassins. Cicero is worried that he might seem disrespectful to them if he implies, as here, that they did not finish the job.

quid indignius...?: In a letter (*ad Att.* 16.11.2), Cicero accepted a suggestion from his friend Atticus to change this into a statement beginning *indignissimum est...* – but for whatever reason never did so. **imposuerit... abiecerit**: Perfect subjunctives because within indirect speech **NLG 314.1** – **eum vivere, (eum) interfectum esse** respectively. **abiecerit** does not imply discard completely – Caesar later, according to Suetonius (*Life of Julius Caesar,* 79.2) and Dio Cassius (44.11.3), sent the *diadema* to the Temple of Jupiter on the Capitol as a dedication. That would indicate a degree of endorsement by Caesar – reason enough for Cicero not to mention it.

Section 87

at etiam – cf. start of § 86. The subject of **iussit** is unspecified, so who caused the inscription in the Fasti of this summary of the event is left in doubt. Dio Cassius (44.11.3, 45.31.4) makes plain that it was Caesar – and many modern ancient historians follow suit. Cicero, who wants to exploit what happened to besmirch Antony, may be echoing the opening of § 86, where Antony was clearly the subject, to imply that he is here, too – but it would take an attentive listener to notice the parallel. **in fastis ad Lupercalia**: (See also note in the previous chapter on **a nobis populoque Romano mandatum**.) The Fasti could be annotated with small letters to commemorate a significant event. But no surviving Fasti bear this annotation, quoted verbatim here by Cicero – it may well be that the order was never carried out, since Caesar died only a month after the Lupercalia.

C. Caesari . . . uti: This quotation from the Fasti is in *oratio obliqua* **NLG 314.1** after **ascribi. dictatori perpetuo**: Caesar had taken office as 'dictator in perpetuity' some time after 26 January 44 BC. It was an inflammatory title, as the original purpose of the position, equipped with absolute powers, was to guide the city through a crisis for no more than a single campaigning season (6 months). Sulla had been appointed dictator (82 BC) and had remained so for 3 years – but this was not a precedent that could be invoked. The purpose of the addition to the Fasti, whoever made it, seems to be to distinguish between the dictatorship and the kingship (of which Caesar accepted the first and refused the second) – so that Caesar could have the power but not the stigma. **populi iussu**: 'At the behest of the people.' Whether Antony or Caesar had been responsible for the addition to the Fasti, the attempt to crown Caesar had to be attributed to the people – just what Cicero expressly denied in the last chapter (**a nobis... id certe non habebas**). Dio Cassius (46.19.5) has an orator, Calenus, claim that Antony was pretending to have authorisation from the people to shame Caesar into abandoning his monarchical intentions – i.e. the very reverse of what Cicero argues here. Plainly there has always been room for profoundly different interpretations. **regnum**: See note on **regem**, § 80. The hatred of kings, or aspiring kings, is taken as read at the end of this chapter. **Caesarem uti noluisse** – sc. *regno*.

iam iam minime miror. . .: This governs the ensuing accusative (**te**) and infinitives (**perturbare, odisse, bibere**). **iam iam** – 'Now indeed'. Cicero is saying that Antony's rabble-rousing is no surprise since Antony is incapable of living in peace, relying on the apparatus of justice. For Antony's taste in companions, see for example § 15; for his drinking, §§ 42, 63, 81.

de die. . . in diem: 'from early in the day. . . daily'. (**in diem** as 'till dawn' is unattested in Cicero, though some editors interpret it so.) *cena*, which would be the time for wine-drinking, would be taken after the ninth hour (i.e. three-quarters of the way through daylight, hours being of unequal length throughout the year, from 45 minutes at the winter solstice to 75 at the summer).

qui locus?: "What refuge. . ." **quae** refers both to the **leges** and to the **iudicia**; it is neuter either because it is taking the gender of the most recent antecedent, or because abstract feminine nouns in compound antecendents can be referred to by a neuter relative pronoun **NLG 250.2**. **quantum in te fuit**: 'As far as lay in your power.' **dominatu regio sustulisti**: Antony had provided Caesar with the excuse to invade Italy (§ 53) and become absolute ruler (in effect, *rex*). At the Lupercalia he was attempting to make that position 'official'. The **dominatus** is Caesar's. **sustulisti** – 'undermined'.

ideone. . . ut. . .: When translating, move **ideo** to **ut** and render 'for this very purpose, that. . .'. **L. Tarquinius**: L. Tarquinius Superbus, the last king of Rome, was deposed in 510/509 BC, by L. Iunius Brutus. **Sp. Cassius**: Spurius Cassius Vi(s)cellinus was three times consul and commander against the Sabines. He was condemned and executed in

485 BC because the agrarian law he had proposed, distributing land among the *plebs* and Latin allies, was construed as a bid for power. **Sp. Maelius**: A rich plebeian whom, when he relieved a food shortage, the *praefectus annonae* (prefect in charge of the corn supply) at the time denounced as fomenting plans for a monarchy. He was killed (439 BC) by the master of the horse, C. Servilius Ahala. **M. Manlius**: M. Manlius Capitolinus, holder of the Capitol against the Gauls, was also prominent in aiding the impoverished *plebs* after the war. He was also condemned for harbouring kingly ambitions and hurled from the Tarpeian Rock (384 BC).

Section 88

sed ad auspicia redeamus: **redeamus** is hortatory subjunctive **NLG 274**, 'let us return'; the **auspicia**, first mentioned in § 80, were those at the consular elections when Dolabella was standing, as was described earlier, and then interrupted in § 84 by the digression on the Lupercalia. **acturus** – 'debate'. Not in the same sense as **egisses** in the next sentence.

tum tu quid egisses?: **egisses** is a potential subjunctive **NLG 280.4**, 'What would you have done then?', like the apodosis of a conditional whose protasis would be something like, 'if Caesar had managed to debate those auspices'.

audiebam: The imperfect matters – 'I kept on hearing'. **quod me... putares esse dicturum**: The subjunctive after **quod** is due to **audiebam** – the reason given in the **quod** clause is part of what Cicero heard **NLG 314.1. ementitis** – passive, though from a deponent. **quibus tamen parere necesse erat**: The use of the indicative here shows that this was not part of what Antony thought, but a parenthetic comment from Cicero. 'Because you thought I was going to speak about the auspices – which, though faked, it was nevertheless necessary to obey.'

sustulit illum diem fortuna rei publicae: sustulit is a technical term for 'took out of the schedule of public business'; **rei publicae** is most likely genitive, though could also be dative, of (dis)advantage **NLG 188.1** or separation **188.2 (d), fortuna** – 'good fortune' – refers to the assassination of Caesar.

num. . . sustulit?: This rhetorical question is sarcastic – two days after Caesar's assassination, Antony recognised Dolabella as his fellow-consul; nothing else had changed.

sed incidi. . . praevertendum est: 'But I have come to that time (i.e. the period after Caesar's murder) which must be considered before (**praevertendum**) the matters on which my speech has embarked (Antony's abuse of the auspices)'. The nominative relative pronoun **quod** has **praevertendum** as its predicate.

quae tua fuga, quae formido. . ., quae. . . desperatio. . .: This triple exclamation is also a way of narrating the immediate aftermath of the assassination, when Antony, as one of Caesar's closest allies, took flight from the scene of the crime and hid himself in his own house. He was allowed to do this because the conspirators, following the arguments of M. Brutus to limit the purge to the dictator alone, had decided to spare him. (Plutarch (*Antony* 14.1) says he disguised himself as a slave.) Cicero vividly imagines this moment from Antony's standpoint, when Antony was unaware that he had not been earmarked as a victim. Cicero might be guessing when he says Antony went to his house (in the Carinae district, some way from the Theatre of Pompey where Caesar was killed). He might more sensibly have escaped to his gardens on the northern edge of the Campus Martius (see Ramsey ad loc.). **beneficio eorum**: 'Through the kindness of those. . .' – **beneficio** is ablative of cause **NLG 219; eorum** refers to the conspirators, who might have been expected to wipe out Caesar's supporters with Caesar. **si sanus esses**: A sideswipe at Antony – the conspirators wanted Antony safe if he was of sound mind; i.e. had they known what his state of mind was, they would not have been so magnanimous.

Section 89

o mea... verissima auguria: Accusative of exclamation **NLG 183**. **frustra** qualifies **verissima** – 'utterly truthful, but uselessly so'.

dicebam – the imperfect is significant, 'I kept saying...'. **illis in Capitolio liberatoribus nostris**: After Caesar's assassination, the conspirators (who had styled themselves 'liberators') walled themselves up on the Capitol, under the guard of D. Brutus's gladiators. Cicero visited them there on the night of 15/16 March to advise that they call a meeting of the senate on the Capitol and take advantage of the disarray among the supporters of Caesar. They failed to do so, and came down after a meeting of the senate on 17 March, called by Antony, had declared an amnesty and Antony had provided his own son as a hostage to the conspirators (see § 90). As Cicero acknowledges, Antony was more than anyone responsible for averting a civil war at this juncture: in addition to Caesar's popular support and the presence in Rome of many of his veterans, on 16 March Caesar's *magister equitum* (i.e. deputy), M. Aemilius Lepidus, reached the city with 6,000 troops, and was eager to storm the conspirators' position. It was thanks to Antony's authority (and, no doubt, his wish to shore it up further) that – for the moment, at least – there was no more blood-letting. Cicero attributes his actions to simple *timor*, fear of a more thorough-going purge by the conspirators. Certainly, Antony's peace-brokering did not last long. **quoad metueres, omnia te promissurum: omnia...promissurum** *(sc. esse)* is accusative and infinive after **dicebam**. The **quoad** clause is in the subjunctive both because it refers to the future **NLG 293 III** and because it is part of what Cicero said **NLG 314.1**.

simul ac = *simulac*. **desisses** – subjunctive to represent a future perfect indicative in *oratio obliqua*, historic sequence **NLG 319 B. similem te futurum tui**: Literally, 'you would be like yourself', i.e. you would show your true colours'. **tui** is genitive.

irent, redirent: 'came and went'.

neque. . . credidi: 'Thus I did not see you either on that day or the next (**neque illo die neque postero**), nor did I believe (**neque credidi**) . . .'. **optimis civibus** – dative, 'for the most upright citizens'. Cicero is not just making a contrast with **importunissimo hoste**, but also alluding to the *optimates* – *populares* split (aristocrats versus people's 'party').

post diem tertium: 'on 17 March', i.e. two days later, by inclusive reckoning. For **post** with the accusative in this phrase, see **NLG 357. in aedem Telluris**: The senate could meet and transact business in any temple; that of Tellus was on the Esquiline, facing the forum, and was near Antony's house. The forum at this moment was occupied by Lepidus's soldiers while the conspirators were still barricaded in the Capitol, just above it; so it would not have been a comfortable location for a meeting of the senate. **et quidem invitus**: 'And unwillingly at that.' **armati obsiderent**: As well as Lepidus's force, many of Caesar's veterans were im Rome. Although disbanded, they still had their weapons and, since they were in the city either to see their old commander off on his Parthian campaign or to claim their allotment of land, the assassination would have aroused more than political resentment.

Section 90

qui tibi. . . fuit!: 'What a day that was for you, Antony!' Antony's conciliation was unexpected (see note on §89, **in Capitolio liberatoribus nostris**).

inimicus subito exstitisti: In *Philippic* 5.19, Cicero recalls how, after he delivered the First Philippic on 2 September, Antony had declared his enmity towards Cicero and commanded him to attend a meeting of the senate on 19 September (*inimicitias mihi denuntiavit; adesse in senatum iussit a.d. XIII Kalendas Octobres*). The First Philippic was designed to turn not just the senate but also Antony's own followers against him. See 'Introduction – Historical Background'.

quod tibi invideris: The (perfect) subjunctive after **quod** is found giving emotional reasons (**NLG 286.1.a** is relevant but not exhaustive); '... because you have done yourself wrong' – by betraying good actions with bad ones.

qui tu vir: 'What a hero....'.

pacem haberemus: Potential subjunctive – 'we would have the peace....'. **obsidem puerum nobilem**: After the meeting of the senate on 17 March, Antony delivered his own son to the conspirators as a pledge of good faith. This was the elder of Antony's two sons by Fulvia, the widow of P. Clodius (see §§ 21 – 2), whom Antony married in 47–46 BC: M. Antonius Antyllus would have been about two at this time. **M. Bambalionis nepotem**: This is a genealogy with a sting – M. Fulvius Bambalio was so-called (from the Greek *bambalein*, 'to stutter') because he was slow-witted and had a speech impediment. Fulvia's mother was not well-born, a fact of which the juxtaposition of her parentage with **nobilem** was intended to jog the listeners' memories.

non diuturnus magister officii: In apposition to **timor** – 'no long-term teacher of what one ought to do'. **ea quae... audacia**: *audacia*, which goes with **ea**, is long postponed. On **audacia**, see note on it in § 44.

etsi – 'and yet' (as in § 47 – see note on **etsi incidamus**). **putabant** –

'people were thinking'. **me quidem dissentiente**: Concessive ablative absolute, 'while I was of a different opinion' **NLG 227. funeri tyranni**: Caesar's funeral took place on 20 March. This is the first place in the Philippics where Cicero uses the word *tyrannus* of Caesar (it returns in §§ 96, 110, 117). The word had the pejorative sense for Romans that it has for us (see note on § 80, **regem**), though originally the Greek (possibly from Lydian) had meant simply a usurper, usually by military force. **si illud funus fuit**: Caesar's friend and correspondent Atticus warned that all was lost if Caesar was granted a public funeral (*ad Att.* 14.14.3). A pyre had been erected in the Campus Martius for the proper cremation, but the corpse never reached it – it was burned inadequately by the mob on a pyre they hastily erected in the forum itself, once they had been stirred up by Antony's oration (see next chapter).

Section 91

tua... cohortatio: sc. *fuit* with each member of the *tricolon. The speech Antony made to the crowd in the forum is reconstructed speculatively by Dio Cassius (44.36–49) and of course by Shakespeare (*Julius Caesar*, III.ii.73), but has not survived. Plutarch's account (*Antony*, 14.3–4; similar in *Brutus*, 20.4–7) might have been based on that of a genuine eyewitness:

> 'Now, it happened that when Caesar's body was carried forth for burial, Antony pronounced the customary eulogy over it in the forum. And when he saw that the people were mightily swayed and charmed by his words, he mingled with his praises sorrow and indignation over the dreadful deed, and at the close of his speech shook on high the garments of the dead, all bloody and tattered by the swords as they were, called those who had wrought such work villains and murderers, and inspired his hearers with such rage that they heaped together

benches and tables and burned Caesar's body in the forum, and then, snatching the blazing faggots from the pyre, ran to the houses of the assassins and assaulted them.'

(Bernadotte Perrin, Loeb, 1923)

The scene was eerily reminiscent of the funeral of P. Clodius, in 52 BC, whose body was given an impromptu cremation in the senate house, thus burning the building down (see below, **semustilatus**). Cicero has no need to narrate what must have been branded on the memories of onlookers.

tu. . . illas faces incendisti: *Hyperbole; Cicero means by his oratory – Antony had benefited from his coach after all (§ 84). **eas quibus semustilatus ille est**: **eas** sc. *faces* (likewise with the next **eas**); **ille** is Caesar. **L. Bellieni domus**: Nothing is known of L. Bellienus other than what can be conjectured from this passage, that he was probably a supporter of the conspirators (though the murder the mob committed, of Helvius Cinna, was the result of mistaken identity: they took him for the praetor and supporter of the conspirators Cornelius Cinna). The destruction of his house was the only collateral damage, despite the attacks described by Cicero here and by Plutarch (above).

tu illos impetus. . . quos nos vi manuque reppulimus. . . in nostras domos immisisti: **quos** refers to **impetus**. **vi manuque** is a natural *hendiadys for 'main force'. The plural **nostras domos** may be because the attackers made for the houses of Brutus and Cassius as well (see Plutarch above, and Suetonius, *Life of Julius Caesar*, 85.1).

idem tamen: 'you, however, also. . .' **quasi fuligine abstersa**: Ablative absolute **NLG 227**. **reliquis diebus**: 'In the days that followed'. **in Capitolio**: Meetings of the senate could be called in the Temple of Capitoline Jupiter. **senatus consulta fecisti**: **fecisti** because Antony was consul, with Dolabella. These **consulta** are mentioned in *Philippic* 3.30 ('two or three decrees made sensibly and in the interests of the republic'). The first decree epitomised here is more specifically described in *Philippic* 1.3: a proposal of Servius Sulpicius, endorsed by Antony, that no resolution or grant of Caesar's should be made public after the Ides of March. This was probably not so much to rescind Caesar's measures as to allow the senate to review them. **ne qua. . . figeretur**: Indirect command **NLG 295.1**, explaining the content of (one of) the decrees; **qua** agreeing with **tabula**, 'any' **NLG 91.1. tabula**: Laws were engraved on bronze tablets and posted on the Capitol or other public places. '. . . that after the Ides of March no notice of any tax exemption nor of any favour should be posted on the Capitol'.

meministi. . . dixeris: de exulibus and **de immunitate** need to be translated with **quid dixeris**. In *Philippic* 1.3, Cicero cites Antony as denying that he brought back any exiles except one (Sextus Cloelius, a supporter of P. Clodius – see § 7), or gave any immunity from taxes.

optimum vero quod. . .: sc. *erat*, 'Indeed the highlight was the fact that. . .'; **quod** here introduces a substantive clause **NLG 299.1**, not a causal one. **dictaturae nomen**: The title 'dictator' was given in the early Republic for a period up to six months to a magistrate when a crisis demanded swift decisions and action. L. Sulla, in 82 BC, was granted it so he could reform the state, without time limit – but retired in 79 BC. In late 49 BC Caesar was awarded it to run elections for the following year, then after the battle of Pharsalus (48 BC) was awarded it again for 12 months, then in 46 BC, after his victory at Thapsus, was granted a 10-year term. Finally, in 44 BC, probably in February, this grant was made life-long – to the utter dismay of his republican opponents. **sustulisti**: Antony's proposal was made soon after Caesar's death and ratified as law in June. It was more cosmetic than Cicero made out: the actual powers of a dictator could, as the emperors were to show, be clothed in other titles.

tantum te cepisse odium regni videbatur: videbatur impersonal, with accusative and infinitive. **regni** indicates how, understandably, the title of dictator became tarnished with the same associations as monarchy (see § 87). **eius omnem... metum tolleres: eius**, objective genitive **NLG 200**, referring to **regni** – 'that you removed all fear of it'.

Section 92

constituta – 'settled', 'secure'. **mihi vero nullo modo**: Another instance of Cicero as Cassandra (§ 89). In fact (*ad Att.* 14.3.2) at the time (early April) Cicero was not concerned about Antony: 'Yet I am inclined to think that he is more occupied with his banquets than with any mischievous designs.' By the end of April, however (*ad Att.* 14.14.2 ff.), Cicero was worried that Caesar's papers, entrusted to Antony by Caesar's widow Calpurnia, were being abused to justify Antony's own proposals.

omnia te gubernante naufragia: 'Every kind of shipwreck with you at the helm.' The ship-of-state *metaphor was cliché enough not to need any prefatory *quasi*.

num... dissimilis: 'Was I wrong, and could he any longer hide his true colours?' The **aut** introduces the explanation of the first rhetorical question. For **dissimilis** here, with genitive **sui**, compare **similem... tui** in § 89.

toto Capitolio tabulae figebantur: toto Capitolio is ablative of place **NLG 228**. The way Antony renegued on the previous resolution, for personal gain, is explored in §§ 93 – 101 (epitomised below).

venibant: From **veneo**, not **venio**. Cicero stresses that Antony was being bribed for his favours. **civitas** = 'citizenship'. Citizenship was prized because it gave access to the career-path offered by the legions and the magistracies. **provinciis totis**: This is not mentioned in the ensuing chapters: in April Antony published a *lex Julia* which granted citizenship to Sicily. It is debated if this particular concession outlasted Antony himself. The plural **provinciis** is almost certainly an exaggeration.

huius domesticis nundinis: huius with a finger pointed at Antony. Cicero makes frequent reference to Antony's graft, his willingness to bestow privileges for cash. Among other words (such as **venibant** above) **nundinae** (and a cognate) occurs three times in this speech (here, §35 and § 115). Cicero particularly wants to contrast the international and enduring deals with their domestic, transient, setting.

Confirmatio 44–114 continues:

Sections 93–96: [Turning to Antony's finances…] Where are the 700 million sesterces listed in the account books of the temple of Ops? And how did you suddenly clear debts of 40 million sesterces, incurring interest on the Ides of March, before the next interest payment on the Kalends of April? Large numbers of privileges were purchased through your agents, with your full knowledge – for instance by Massilia [modern Marseilles]. The most remarkable decree, however, was the one restoring to King Deiotarus his territory in Galatia. [King Deiotarus; a tetrarch of Galatia, had appropriated the entire territory, murdering his own daughter and son-on-law in the process. He had offered help to Cicero during the latter's governorship of Cilicia (in 51 BC) and supported Pompey during his campaign against Mithridates of Pontus. As a result he was rewarded with an extension of his territory and the title 'King'. He sided with Pompey during the Civil War, then asked for and was granted a pardon by Caesar after Pharsalus (48 BC), but Caesar removed some of his domains (including part of Galatia and Armenia). Caesar stayed with Deiotarus in 47 BC. The latter later (45 BC) was accused of trying to poison his guest. Cicero delivered his defence of Deiotarus in Caesar's own house (*pro Rege Deiotaro*). Caesar had still not delivered a verdict when he died.] How strange that Caesar should have taken things away from him in life and given them back in death. King Deiotarus's ambassadors had signed a promissory note worth 10 million sesterces in the quarters of Fulvia [Antony's wife]. When the king heard of Caesar's death, however, he took matters into his own hands and seized his lost territory himself, before he had to pay the sum borrowed. No lawyer could enforce the contract.

Sections 97–99: Money has piled up at Antony's house through the sale of signatures [purported to be Caesar's]. Such was the blindness of his greed that the Cretans were remitted tribute, as if by will of Caesar, 'after the governorship of the proconsul M. Brutus' – though Brutus had not been allotted the governorship until after Caesar's death. Exiles who Caesar had wanted to recall were lumped together with those you wanted to recall – so many that few are left abroad. Your inconsistency is nowhere more apparent than in the treatment of your exiled uncle, C.

Antonius [see summary of sections 55b – 58 above], whom you delayed recalling, to whom you then promised the censorship and membership of the agrarian board only to disappoint him, and whose daughter, Antonia, you spurned for another woman [Fulvia] and divorced on a trumped-up charge of adultery with Dolabella [a notorious womaniser – Cicero was his father-in-law].

Section 100

ad chirographa: These are Caesar's private papers, as mentioned in § 97–8; see also note on § 92, **mihi vero nullo modo**. The Greek word from which the Latin is taken means 'hand-written document'. **redeamus** – hortatory subjunctive **NLG 274**, after the digression on Antony's uncle.

cognitio = 'investigation', as is soon explained: the senate decided that Antony and a committee should investigate Caesar's transactions (**ut. . . de Caesaris actis cum consilio cognosceretis**).

acta enim Caesaris: acta are the decisions proposed by, in this case, Caesar and then in some form ratified (usually by the senate); 'transactions' would be a valid translation. **pacis causa**: 'For the sake of peace', to be taken with **confirmata sunt**. After Caesar's death, the senate deemed the best way to keep order was to confirm the dictator's transactions – which then raised the question of what he could be said to have 'transacted' and gave Antony, possessor of Caesar's papers, his opportunity to claim certain decisions of his own (says Cicero) as Caesar's.

quae quidem Caesar egisset: The subjunctive here is generic, expressing a limitation **NLG 283.3 b**, as shown by the **quidem** – 'but those which Caesar had indeed authorised'. It is also in implicit *oratio obliqua*, after **confirmata sunt NLG 314.1**. The word order in what follows is distorted for effect (see style note), from *non ea quae Antonius Caesarem egisse dixisset*.

erumpunt: Present because Cicero treats these *acta* as still emerging – 'From where do they keep bursting forth...?'

at sic placuerat ut... cognosceretis: With **placuerat**, sc. *senatui*. The **sic** goes closely with the **ut**: 'Yet the senate had decided that....'. This refers to a decree of the senate (*senatus consultum*) which Cicero mentions in his letters (*ad Att.* 16.16c.2), that the consuls should carry out an investigation (**cognitio**) into Caesar's decisions, decrees and dealings, starting from 1 June. A law, passed on 2 June, reaffirmed this. The same letter cites one matter which was adjudicated by the consuls and their advisers, after that date. **cognosceretis** here is plural because Antony was to act with his fellow-consul, Dolabella. **cum consilio** – 'in council'.

quod fuit consilium...?: Cicero's *rhetorical question strongly implies that Antony never called the council, though as noted above, it did meet, and after 1 June. **quem** – accusative of **quis. convocasti** for *convocavisti*, **exspectasti** for *exspectavisti* **NLG 116.1. quas Kalendas Iunias...?**: Literally 'what Kalends of June did you await?', i.e. 'what attention did you pay to that Kalends of June?'. Antony produced many of his fake Caesar signatures in April, before he left Rome on a tour of the veteran colonies of Campania (see next sentence).

an eas ad quas...: **an** introduces an insistent additional question **NLG 162.4 a.**; **eas ad quas** = 'those (Kalends) on which'. **peragratis veteranorum coloniis**: Antony went to Campania in execution of a law (*lex de coloniis in agros deducendis*) passed, it seems, earlier in April, under which he was to settle veterans in colonies with land grants. At the time of Caesar's assassination there were large numbers of his veterans in Rome, and settling them in Campania was a way both of removing them from the city and of cementing their loyalty to Caesar's (and thus Antony's) cause. **stipatum armis** – 'hedged about with weaponry'.

o praeclaram illam percursationem: Accusative of exclamation **NLG 183. mense Aprili atque Maio**: Ablative of time within which **NLG 231. tum cum... conatus es: cum** with the indicative **NLG 288.1** indicates the point in time at which something occurs (reinforced often by **tum**). **Capuam**: Accusative of destination **NLG 182.1 a**, with **deducere** (which retains its sense of leading to a place). Capua had already become a colony in 59 BC, under a law of Caesar's (*de Bello Civ.* i.14.4). Cicero, as we learn in § 102, warned Antony that he could not install a second colony where one already existed.

quem ad modum... scimus: quem ad modum introduces an indirect question, depending on **scimus. paene non abieris**: Capua (*Philippic* 12.7) blocked Antony and, Cicero suggests, all but laid hands on him. When Octavian was touting for support against Antony in October 44 BC, Capua cooperated with alacrity.

Section 101

cui... urbi: Capua.

utinam: + subjunctive (**conere**), 'would that', or less antiquatedly, 'how I wish...' **NLG 279.1. conere**: 'try (to do what you threaten)'. In the next chapter Cicero describes how Antony encroached on Capua's domains for his colony at Casilinum (see note there on **perstrinxisti**). **ut aliquando illud 'paene' tollatur**: This refers to the **paene** in the phrase **paene non abieris**, two sentences ealier – i.e. next time, may Antony not have any escape.

at quam nobilis est...: Present tense because under current scrutiny. This does not work in English, so translate as 'was'.

quid... proferam?: quid = 'why?' **proferam** is probably deliberative subjunctive **NLG 277** rather than future.

tua ista detrimenta sunt, illa nostra: tua. . . detrimenta, objective – 'harm to you' (as **nostra**, 'to us'). **ista** points backwards to the previous sentence, **illa** further back to **illa peregrinatio**, whose effects are explained in the next sentence. **sunt** is present because the harm is still being felt. **agrum Campanum. . . dividebas**: This sentence's structure breaks down (*anacoluthon) after *qui*, since the relative should have something to do with the clause **tamen infligi. . . putabamus** – i.e. be subject of a clause such as *non sine magno rei publicae vulnere datus est* [Ramsey], 'which was parcelled out at great cost to the Republic'. Instead it is left stranded, being only subject of **eximebatur**, till **hunc** picks it up its antecedent again, the **agrum Campanum** (object of **dividebas**). **cum** with indicative to pinpoint a particular moment **NLG 288.1. tamen** offsets the **ut**. Translate:'At the time when the territory of Campania was being exempted from producing revenue for the state, albeit to be allocated to the troops, we still thought a great wound...: <for> this very territory you proposed to distribute (**dividebas**, imperfect) ...'. In 211 BC, the area of Campania round Capua, recaptured from Hannibal, was confiscated and made into **ager publicus** (cf. **arationes** later in this chapter, 'public land'): those who enjoyed the use of it were in effect tenants of the Roman government, to which they paid either a proportion of their produce or a fee per head of livestock. By turning this land over to colonisation in 59 BC, Caesar sacrificed the revenue (**vectigalia**) from it, since the colonists were freeholders. The soldiers who benefited in this way were first of all Pompey's veterans from the wars against Mithridates of Pontus, covered by Caesar's legislation, then Caesar's own veterans in 45 BC. Antony made two settlements of veterans in that year; the second, on a larger scale, in June, is probably what Cicero refers to here.

mimos dico et mimas: Cicero is giving an alternative description of the **conlusores** and **compransores** in the previous sentence. **dico** is 'I mean'.

quid iam querar...?: 'Why should I complain...?', deliberative subjunctive again (cf. **quid... proferam** above) **NLG 277**.

agro Leontino: Leontini, on Sicily, lies north of Syracuse. **arationes**: Arable land owned by the state (see note on **ager publicus** above – that would include grazing land also). **Campana et Leontina**: Singular adjectives as if agreeing individually with **aratio. ferebantur** – 'were said to be'.

medico tria milia iugerum: sc. *dedisti*. **iugerum** is an irregular form (heteroclite) of the genitive plural from *iugerum* (2/3 acre), after **milia NLG 80.5**. The identity of the **medicus** is unknown. **quid, si te sanasset?**: **quid** sc. *ei dedisses*. **sanasset** for *sanavisset* **NLG 116.1**; 'cured you (of your folly)'.

rhetori duo: sc. *milia iugerum dedisti*. The teacher is Sex. Clodius, of § 43 and § 85. The total grant on the Leontine plain of 5,000 iugera represents a sixth of all its land (*2 Verr* 3.113). A veteran could expect 10 iugera (see Cicero's calculation in *ad Att.* 2.16.1).

ad iter Italiamque redeamus: See note on **redeamus** in § 100 – another return from a digression. Cicero is assiduous in guiding his listeners.

Section 102

Casilinum: Accusative of destination **NLG 182.1 a**, again with **deducere** (see note on **Capuam** in § 100). Casilinum is a town in Campania some three miles north of Capua.

consuluisti me per litteras de Capua tu quidem: The letters communicating Antony's consultation of Cicero are not extant. **de Capua tu quidem** admits that Antony's question was not about Casilinum. **respondissem**: Past potential subjunctive **NLG 280.4**, 'I would have answered'.

possesne: This introduces as indirect the question that Antony posed to Cicero in his consultation (**consuluisti**). **-ne** is the equivalent of *num* when introducing an indirect question **NLG 300.1 b. esset** is subjunctive because in *oratio obliqua* **NLG 314.1. eo** = 'to that place'.

auspicato: This virtual adverb is an impersonal ablative absolute **NLG 227** from *auspico*, a less common variant of *auspicor*. Cicero's reasoning is that the once the auspices had been taken to confirm the foundation of the colony, its boundaries were sacrosanct; it could, however, absorb new members. **dum esset incolumis**: 'provided that it was intact' – if a colony were seriously damaged and depopulated, it could require refounding. **iure deduci**: The emphasis is on **iure** – '(I said that) it was not right (for a new colony) to be founded'.

rescripsi – the word for an expert reply to a consultation. 'I gave my opinion that...'

omni auspiciorum iure turbato: Ablative absolute **NLG 227**, more naturally translated as if present – 'in defiance of the all the law on auspices'. **quo erat paucis annis ante deducta**: sc. *colonia*. **paucis annis ante**, 'a few years before', uses the ablative of measure of difference (see note on **multis ante mensibus**, § 81). **ut vexillum tolleres**: It was customary to hoist a military standard at the foundation of a colony in recognition of the role colonies had once played as Roman outposts. It was doubly appropriate here because the colonists were retired soldiers. The **ut** stresses that Antony's specific purpose was to found a new colony. **aratrum circumduceres**: This alludes to the ritual of ploughing a furrow round the perimeter of a future fortification (leaving gaps for the gates).

portam Capuae paene perstrinxisti: This is clearly *hyperbole, but Cicero is indicating how Antony attempted a form of reprisal on Capua for its chilly reception of him (§ 100) by appropriating its land.

Section 103

ab hac perturbatione religionum: ab = 'after'. Cicero is referring back to the phrase **omni auspiciorum iure turbato** in the previous chapter; **perturbatione** echoes **turbato** and **religiones** ('religious scruples', as § 48) corresponds to **ius auspiciorum. advolas** – historic present **NLG 259.3. in M. Varronis... villam Casinatem**: The **in** governs **villam**. M. Terentius Varro (116–27 BC), one of Rome's greatest scholars, also had a public career under Pompey – fighting Sertorius in Spain, then the pirates and after that becoming joint governot of Hispania Ulterior till 49 BC. When Pompey's forces were defeated at Ilerda, Varro surrendered his province to Caesar. He was in Pompey's camp before the battle of Pharsalus (48 BC) and may have suffered confiscations as a result of that. Nevertheless, by 45 BC he had been restored to favour, as Caesar gave him the responsibility of procuring and classifying Greek and Latin books for a library in Rome (Suetonius, *Life of Julius Caesar*, 44.2). He was outlawed by Antony in 43 BC, but outlived the Civil War and continued his astonishingly prolific output. Although only works on the Latin language and agriculture survive, a catalogue of his writings shows that he ventured into history, geography, medicine, music, architecture, philosophy, satire and more. **villam Casinatem**: Casinum lay on the via Latina, about half way between Rome and Naples. On the hill above it St. Benedict, c. 530, set his monastery of Monte Cassino. In Varro's *de Re Rustica* (3.5.9–17), a conversation piece taking place in 54 BC but actually written from 37 BC onwards, the author describes his aviary, fish ponds, rotunda and other delights; presumably Antony's occupation was a transient one.

quo ore?: 'With what cheek?' This use of **os** resembles 'face' in English. It is particularly common in comedy.

eodem... quo in heredum... praedia: sc. *iure*, **ore** with **eodem**. The **in** governs **praedia**, and a verb such as *intrasti* is understood from the sense of **advolas. heredum** refers to the rightful heirs whom Antony displaced – in §40 – 1, we hear how Antony secured inheritances from strangers; **L. Rubrius** (otherwise unknown) passed over his nephew in Antony's favour. In § 74 we are told that the heirs of L. Rubrius successfully petitioned Caesar to stop Antony from holding an auction of their estate (presumably on the grounds that Rubrius's will was in some way invalid). **inquies** is the future of *inquis*. **L. Turseli**: Likewise unknown, except for this speech and his role as testator to Antony's benefit.

et si ab hasta, valeat hasta: sc. *emisti*. The **hasta** was the notice of an auction (probably in origin the advertisement of war booty on sale) and hence, by *metonymy, the auction itself. Cicero explores the possibility that Varro's property was confiscated after Pharsalus (see above note on **Varro**). **valeat** and then **valeant** are jussive subjunctive **NLG 275.1**. **valeant. . . liberavisti: tabulae** has two senses: (1) the official records of sale (2) the accounts showing them. Sense (1) goes with **valeant**, sense (2) with **quibus debuisti**. The second relative clause, **non quibus. . .**, refers to **tuae. modo** means 'provided that (they are)' **NLG 310 II**. 'Let the records stand, provided they are Caesar's and not yours; those under which you were a debtor, not those by which you wriggled free'. Antony's miraculous escape from debt was dealt with in § 93.

Varronis quidem Casinatem fundum: The lack of joining word to the previous sentence here creates a strong contrast – '<Whatever else might have been up for sale,> as for Varro's farm at Casinum. . .'. The whole phrase is displaced from **quis dicit venisse? venisse** from *veneo*. **praeconis**: The herald announcing the sale, approximating to our 'auctioneer'.

misisse te dicis Alexandriam qui emeret: sc. *aliquem* as object of **misisse**. Again, adversative *asyndeton, to emphasise that Antony's own admission is evidence against an auction. **Alexandream** is accusative of destination **NLG 182.1 a**. For the form, see § 48 and note. After Pharsalus (June 48 BC Julian date), Caesar pursued Pompey to Egypt. Despite Pompey's murder, Caesar remained there backing Cleopatra VII in her conflict with her brother, Ptolemy XIII, and from December 48 till June 47 was incommunicado, not returning to Rome until October that year. Antony would have sent his messenger to Caesar on the assumption that Varro's farm had been confiscated by the state – a supposition which Cicero says in the next chapter is contradicted by Caesar's own communications. **emeret** is subjunctive of purpose **NLG 282.2**, 'to buy (sc. the farm)'.

ipsum: i.e. *Caesarem*. **magnum fuit**: 'It would have been a long undertaking....'. As, in fact, it was – though Cicero seems to be suggesting that Antony's impatience was unreasonable. The indicative **fuit** replaces a potential subjunctive, as in phrases like *longum est, difficile est* **NLG 271.1 b**.

Section 104

nullius autem salus curae pluribus fuit: curae is predicative dative **NLG 191.2**. 'Indeed, nobody had more people concerned for their well-being'. Cicero's argument is that, since so many were looking out for Varro, the chances of nobody hearing that harm had come to him or his property were minuscule.

si etiam scripsit ad te Caesar ut redderes: 'If in fact Caesar wrote to you (telling you) to restore it (the villa)'. **ut** introduces an indirect command **NLG 295.1** after **scripsit**. This indicates not necessarily that Caesar knew Antony had seized it, but certainly that he wished Varro not to be deprived of it.

remove. . . quos videmus: Cicero gestures at Antony's thugs (see note on § 46 **cum. . . meminisses**) who were in attendance. Bodyguards were associated with warlords; but Cicero had himself used bodygruards at the time of the Catilinarian conspiracy, in 63 BC, and Antony had the additional lesson of Caesar's assassination to ponder: Caesar had dismissed his own Spanish bodyguard when the Senate took an oath to preserve his safety (Suetonius, *Life of Julius Caesar* 86.1, 84.2). The imperative **remove** is the equivalent of a conditional, cf. 'seek and you will find'. Keeping two main ideas when one is, in thought, subordinate to the other is called parataxis. **iam intelleges** – 'then you will understand'. **causam** – not so much 'cause' as 'circumstances'. '... the circumstances of Caesar's auction were one thing, those of your thoughtless complacency another'. **confidentia** could have positive or negative connotations.

non enim te dominus modo... arcebit: The list **amicus, vicinus, hospes, procurator** contains people – with the exception of a **procurator**, or agent authorised by the owner to act on his behalf – who would have had no legal jurisdiction over Antony. Yet, Cicero claims, even they would keep Antony out of Varro's home. **illis sedibus... arcebit** – 'will keep you from that dwelling'; **sedibus** is ablative of separation **NLG 214.2; sedes** is sometimes used in the plural for a single home.

o tecta ipsa misera: Cicero addresses the house itself (**tecta** is vocative), then quotes, from a tragedy of unknown authorship, a fragment he gives more fully in *de Officiis* 1.139 (*o domus antiqua, heu quam dispari dominare domino* – 'ancient house, alas, what a different owner you are owned by'). He then interrupts himself. **quamquam quo modo iste dominus?**: sc. *est* – 'though how is that fellow an "owner"?' **sed tamen quam ab dispari tenebantur**: The sentence resumes, with a strongly adversative **sed tamen** and without **domino** – 'but rather by what a different *individual* they were possessed'.

studiorum... deversorium: illud refers to the **tecta**, but is attracted to the gender of **deversorium NLG 246.5**. The latter is more appropriate for **libidinum** than for **studiorum**, so some conjecture a noun has dropped out after **studiorum** – but the very violence of the *zeugma reinforces Cicero's point, and gives **deversorium** real punch. **voluit** – sc. *esse*.

Section 105

quae... quae... quae... litteris mandebantur: These **quae**s are all exclamatory: each requires a different noun to be supplied in translation (e.g. 'What words were said, what thoughts entertained, what works entrusted to literary form!').

iura... doctrinae: This verbless sentence lends substance to the various *quae*s. Varro asserted (as cited by Aulus Gellius, *Attic Nights* 3.10) that by the time he entered the twelfth hebdomad of his age (i.e. when 78) he had already completed 70 hebdomads of books (i.e. 490); this in a work on the significance of the number 7. He also remarked that many of these were lost at the time of his proscription, which introduces a note of doubt. Among writings whose titles we know are a work on civil law (in 15 volumes), one on human and divine antiquities (in 41 volumes) and one on philosophy (in 3 volumes). **omnis sapientiae ratio omnisque doctrinae**, however, meaning 'the system (**ratio**) of all philosophy and all learning' [Ramsey], could refer to his output as a whole (and more likely does so).

at vero te inquilino... versabantur: te inquilino – a form of ablative absolute, in the absence of a present participle from *sum* **NLG 227.1. inquilinus** is used for one who resides without ownership; Cicero rubs this in with **non enim domino**, flogging the horse from the previous chapter (**quamquam quo modo iste dominus?**). **personabant omnia** – 'everywhere echoed'. **madebant parietes** –

sc. *vino*. **versabantur**, unlike the other verbs, completes its clause to provide a stronger end for the whole sentence. **pueri ingenui cum meritoriis**: Here, as with **scorta inter matres familias**, Cicero wants to display the corrupting power of Antony. **matres familias** = 'mothers of families', **familias** being an archaic form of the genitive **NLG 21.2 a**.

Casino salutatum... interamna: The places are in the ablative, denoting place whence – without a preposition for towns **NLG 229.1 a**. Aquinum lay about 7 miles west, Interamna about 6 miles south of Casinum. **salutatum** is supine of purpose **NLG 340.1**. The *salutatio* was the morning ritual when *clientes*, potential or actual, would come to pay their respects to their *patronus*. The *patronus* was expected to acknowledge his visitors in some way, preferably with favours: a Roman version of *noblesse oblige*.

admissus est nemo: Cicero states this baldly, as an ill-mannered snub, and with the suggestion that Antony could not reveal the débris from his antics. It might, however, have been for reasons of security: many of the townships outside Rome (*municipia*) were sympathetic to Brutus and Cassius rather than to Caesar (as in § 107).

iure id quidem: sc. *factum est*. The 'rightness' is that nobody was able to pay respects to Antony; if they had done so, they would have been bestowing the recognition of worth (**insignia dignitatis**) on an utter scoundrel (**homini turpissimo**). **obsolefiebant** – imperfect indicative where we might have expected a potential subjunctive, to underline that honours proffered to Antony, both those he received and those which never reached him, were degraded. **obsolefio** is a word not previously attested; it may have been coined her by Cicero.

Section 106

cum inde Romam... ad Aquinum accederet: Cicero moves on from Antony's tenancy of Varro's villa to his return to Rome – and turns away from addressing Antony. Aquinum (see also note on it in last chapter) lay on the via Latina (as below, of the Aquinates, **in via habitabant**), and therefore the route to Rome. **magna sane multitudo**: *magna sane* = 'a naturally large', because of the high population.

at iste operta lectica: at iste is immediately disapproving – 'But that fellow, if you please'. **operta lectica** here contrasts with the **aperta lectica** of § 58, in which Antony ostentatiously rode with his mistress Cytheris. It is possible, certainly after his indulgence, simply that Antony was unwell, even if not **mortuus**.

stulte Aquinates: sc. *fecerunt*. They should have known better than to expect correct etiquette from Antony.

quid Agnanini: sc. *fecerunt*, again. **qui... salutarent: qui** is connecting relative **NLG 251.6**. Agnania was on a ridge above the *via Latina* (**devii**), about 33 miles west of Aquinum. Hence the inhabitants had to come down the hill (**descenderunt**) to greet Antony. **tamquam si esset consul**: 'As if he (really) were consul'. Antony of course was one, but lacked the deportment. In § 10, Cicero calls him **ille nullo modo consul.**

incredibile dictu: The supine **dictu** is in the ablative (of specification **NLG 340.2**) – 'Incredible to say'. **inter omnes constabat**: A common idiom for 'everyone agreed'. **praesertim cum** – 'even though'. **Mustelam et Laconem**: Cicero omits their *praenomina*, as a mark of disdain. In an earlier draft which Atticus had seen, he had omitted their names altogether – but, prompted by Atticus asking who they were, he added them: 'Mr Weasel' and 'Mr Spartan' [Ramsey]. Cicero describes them as the leader of Antony's ruffians and a heavy toper, respectively (*ad Att.* 16.11.3).

Section 107

quid ego... commemorem...?: 'Why should I mention...?' **commemorem** is deliberative subjunctive **NLG 277**. This mention of the Sidicini (a Latin people) and Puteolani (the inhabitants of Puteoli, modern Pozzuoli) is a digression from Antony's journey, as the main town of the Sidicini, Teanum, lay about 25 miles south-east of Casinum, and the town of Puteoli even further. These purported outbursts of Antony would most likely have taken place during his Campanian excursion (§ 101 ff.).

C. Cassium et Brutos patronos adoptasset: adoptasset for *adoptavisset* **NLG 116.1**. The subjunctive is because the reason is part of Antony's invective (**invectus est**), not a comment from Cicero **NLG 286.1**. **patronos**: The governing *decuriones* of towns could nominate a prominent Roman as their **patronus** in gratitude for services rendered; he then became their representative at Rome. Thus, Capua named Cicero its **patronus** after he had quashed the Catilinarian conspiracy. This relationship could pass down the generations – Antony was hereditary **patronus** of Bononia, modern Bologna. **C. Cassium et Brutos**: Caesar's assassins, C. Cassius Longinus, M. Junius Brutus and Decimus Junius Brutus (not related). The removal of Caesar was supported by the aristocracies in the *municipia* (*ad Fam.* 11.2.1) who considered him, as the assassins did, a tyrant.

magno studio... cliens esse: sc. *C. Cassium et Brutos patronos adoptaverunt*. The ablatives in this sentence (including **vi et armis**) are all causal **NLG 219** – 'as a result of...'. **iudicio** = 'discernment'. **non, ut te et Basilum, vi et armis**: After the **ut** sc. *patronos alii adoptaverunt*. **vi et armis** is a regular *hendiadys for 'force of arms'. L. Minucius Basilus was a *patronus* of Picenum and Sabinum, 'a foul blot on the age' (*de Officiis* 3.74). **et alios vestri similes...**: This continues from the accusatives **te et Basilum. vestri** is genitive **NLG 84** after **similes. velit** – potential subjunctive, 'would wish' **NLG 280.2. non modo** – 'not to speak of' (cf. *nedum*). **illorum** stands for a second relative, *quorum*. '(They did this), indeed, out of great devotion, discernment, goodwill and affection, not (as others did) in the case of you and Basilus, as a result of armed force – or as in the case of others like you (both), whom nobody would want as their clients, let alone want to be client of.'

interea dum tu abes: This 'meanwhile' covers the entire period of Antony's absence in Campania up to his return to Rome. **abes** is present, as normal after **dum** meaning 'while' when accompanied by a perfect main verb **NLG 293.1** – 'while you were away'. **qui dies ille conlegae tui fuit**: cf. the opening of § 90; **qui** is exclamatory. Here the day belonged to Dolabella (**conlegae tui** in the consulship). Some editors read the more natural *tuo*, dative of advantage **NLG 188.1. cum** + indicative because pinpointing a particular moment **NLG 288.1. A. quod venerari solebas bustum**: Dolabella late during April levelled Caesar's memorial in the forum (**bustum** is a tomb, the word serving as a subtle reminder from Cicero that Caesar was no god), as narrated in *Philippic* 1.5. **quod venerari solebas** attributes to Antony an attachment to the tomb which he might have felt as a loyal supporter of Caesar, but not for the monument itself – Antony had himself executed the man who put it up. Dolabella, by demolishing the tomb, advertised his readiness to back the conspirators; soon, however, he was even readier to back Antony, who proposed his governorship of Syria to the senate and shared with him the looted contents of the treasury of Ops (§ 93, *ad Att.* 14.18.1).

ut constabat inter eos: For **constabat**, see note on **inter omnes constabat**, § 106. **qui una fuerunt**: 'who were together (with you)', i.e. somewhere in Campania. **concidisti** – 'you collapsed'.

quid evenerit postea nescio: 'As to what happened next, I am not certain.' Cicero alludes to Dolabella's change of side. **metum credo valuisse et arma**: A vague phrase, implying a threat from Antony – **metum…et arma** is best taken as another *hendiadys, for 'fear of armed threat'. Since he knew the real reason why Dolabella defected and detested him for it (*ad Att.* 16.15.1), this **nescio** seems unwontedly tactful of Cicero – Dolabella's marriage (after his own fashion) to Cicero's daughter Tullia meant that Dolabella had a hostage of a kind.

conlegam quidem de caelo detraxisti: *conlegam* refers to Dolabella. **de caelo detraxisti** is 'the reverse of "extolling to the skies"' [Ramsey], i.e. 'knocked down from his position of high esteem'. **tui… sui**: Genitives of **tu** and **se**, dependent on **similis** and then **dissimilis**.

Section 108

qui vero…, quae…!: Exclamatory **qui**, 'what a return…, what a commotion…!' **inde** – i.e. from Puteoli (previous chapter). **Romam**, accusative of end of motion **NLG 182.1**, is used with the noun **reditus** just as we would say 'return *to* Rome'. This was probably mid-May; Antony was accompanied by his armed supporters.

memineramus… videramus: memineramus, from *memini*, means 'we remembered', i.e. is not truly pluperfect – unlike **videramus**. **Cinnam**: L. Cornelius Cinna, consul first in 87 BC, was expelled from Rome after a struggle against his opponents, above all Sulla (see next note), but took Rome by force later that year and kept his hold on power by being reappointed consul annually. In 84 BC, he embarked on campaign and was killed in a mutiny. His history was written by his enemies, who portrayed him as a tyrant. **Sullam**: L. Cornelius Sulla Felix filled the power vacuum left by Cinna, becoming Dictator (see note on § 87, **dictatori perpetuo**); in 82 – 1 BC, his infamous proscriptions purged Rome of his adversaries. Cicero had begun his legal career in the time of Sulla, when he defended Sex. Roscius against a charge of patricide in 80 BC. **modo** – 'recently'.

fortasse gladii: sc. *erant*: These **gladii** are those of the bodyguards (as is clear from a very similar passage in *Philippic* 5.17); Cicero's point is that Antony's henchmen are far more obtrusive than those of his predecessors. **absconditi** – 'sheathed'. **ita** = *tam*.

ista vero. . .est!: The word order is, *vero quae et quanta ista barbaria est*. **barbaria** conjures up the savagery of foreigners, **barbari**. Cicero is probably making particular reference to the archers, mentioned in § 112, of the semi-nomadic Ituraean tribe, widespread in Syria and northern Palestine.

agmine quadrato: The marching formation whereby the column would form a rectangle encasing the baggage train. The idea is that Antony's men were in a state of alert. This was how Cicero describes them as being before this meeting of the senate on 19 September (*Philippic* 5.20) – see 'Introduction – Historical Background'. **cum gladiis**: i.e. with swords at the ready, not **absconditi. sequuntur**: The subject is 'men', left vague. A letter from Brutus and Cassius to Antony (*ad Fam.* xi.2) states the conspirators' concern at the large number of veterans – loyal to Caesar and thus to Antony – congregating in Rome. Appian (*Civil Wars*, iii.5) says Antony kept adding to his bodyguard, consisting of ex-centurions, until it reached 6,000.

scutorum lecticas: 'Litters full of shields', genitive for contents (oddly, not given a grammatical name as such, but exactly as in English). In *Philippic* 5.18, Cicero recalls this use of litters and declares it was not for concealment but to save Antony's *familiares* the trouble of portering them.

atque his iam inveteratis: his means 'these measures (for his self-protection)' taken by Antony. The phrase is an ablative absolute. **consuetudine**: ablative of cause **NLG 219**.

Kalendis Iuniis: The first meeting of the senate after the 'spring recess' [Ramsey].

Section 109

Cicero turns to the ways in which Antony abused his position as Caesar's 'executor' (see note at start of §92) to suit his own ends.

at iste... effecit: The logic of this sentence is, 'Antony didn't need a senate and so far from missing us in our absence was delighted because he could get up to mischief'. **qui... non egeret**: Causal subjunctive **NLG 283.3.a. quemquam** sc. *senatum*. **et potius**: This corrects **neque desideravit; statimque** then answers the **neque**, since it has now been superseded by the positive **laetatus est. discessu** – the scattering referred to at the end of § 108. **mirabilia facinora**: Witheringly sarcastic.

qui... defendisset: qui is not the connecting relative here but introduces a relative clause. The subjunctive is concessive **NLG 283.3.b**, 'although he had defended...', i.e. argued for their genuineness and that they be respected. **chirographa**: Caesar's manuscript documents, already referred to by this word in § 100 (where see note). **lucri sui causa** – 'for his own profit'. **easque praeclaras**: 'Including highly respected ones'. **ut rem publicam concutere posset**: Cicero's examples do not so much support the claim that Antony's aim was to harm the Republic as that he wished to accrue advantages for himself.

numerum annorum provinciis prorogavit: provinciis ('<tenure in> provinces') is more likely dative of advantage **NLG 188**, usual after

prorogo, than an ablative of place **NLG 288**. A law passed by the tribuni plebis prolonged Antony's period of office as proconsul, contrary to Caesar's own measures (*contra acta Caesaris* – *Philippic* 5.7).

cum – concessive/adversative **NLG 309.3**, 'although'. **actorum Caesaris defensor**: Cicero's point is that Antony, who had been entrusted with Caesar's papers and had used them to justify actions of his own (§§ 93 – 4), should not at the same time have been abolishing Caesar's laws or not honouring his legacies (grouped under the term **acta**). **in publicis... in privatis rebus...**: This is a small table of contents – Cicero will go on to speak of **res publicae** (laws) and then **res privatae** (wills).

nihil est lege gravius: *Philippic* 1.18 asks, 'Is there anything which you can call the "deeds" of a man <in government>... as properly as a law?'

leges alias... sine promulgatione sustulit, alias ut tolleret promulgavit: **promulgatio** was the posting of any bill to be discussed a *trinundinum* ahead of the assembly at which it was to be ratified or rejected by vote. Since market days (**nundinae**) occurred every eight days, this was a period of a little over three weeks. Antony has been repealing some of Caesar's legislation (the **alias leges**) without promulgating the laws with which he was intending to replace them, but has also given the requisite advanced notice (understand **novas leges** with **promulgavit**) in order to repeal other parts of Caesar's legislation (**alias ut tolleret**). Cicero gives examples of both practices in *Philippic* 1.19. His point here is that Antony observed protocol only insofar as it suited him.

testamentum: Caesar's will, which had been entrusted to the Vestal Virgins for safe keeping was read out in Antony's house. Suetonius (*Life of Julius Caesar*, 83.1) describes this and the provisions the will made. Antony could have gone through due process to declare the will null and void (**irritum**), but instead (more characteristically) achieved the same end by riding roughshod over its provisions – obstructing Octavian when he came to claim his inheritance and emptying the estate of its artistic contents (see below). **infimis civibus:** 'In the case of the humblest citizens' – dative of advantage **NLG 188.1.**

signa, tabulas quas. . .: quas refers to both the **signa** and the **tabulas NLG 235.B.1. cum hortis. . .:** These gardens, in the south-west of Rome across the Tiber, were Cleopatra's residence in Rome from 46 to early 44 BC. **in hortos Pompeianos:** Pompey's gardens, in the north of Rome, confiscated by Caesar, were sold to Antony at auction in 47 BC. **in villam Scipionis:** The villa of Metellus Scipio, Pompey's father-in-law, mentioned already in § 42, was confiscated after he was defeated by Caesar at the battle of Thapsus (46 BC) and committed suicide.

Section 110

in Caesaris memoria diligens: Cicero pours further scorn on Antony's 'cultivation' of Caesar's memory – neither has he respected Caesar's wishes, nor has he taken up the opportunity provided by the divine privileges granted Caesar during his lifetime (see also Suetonius, *Life of Julius Caesar*, 76.1; Dio Cassius, 44.6) to serve him in a religious capacity. **tu illum amas mortuum:** A deliberately unappealing phrase.

quem is honorem maiorem. . .?: 'What greater honour. . .?' **quem** is the interrogative adjective **NLG 90.2.** The honour is explained by the **ut** clause which follows **NLG 295.2. pulvinar, simulacrum, fastigium, flaminem:** In celebration of thanksgiving (**supplicatio**), the images of the gods and goddesses were placed on sacred couches (**pulvinaria**) inside or, often, outside the temple and offered a sacred banquet (the whole ceremony being called *lectisternium*). **simulacrum**

is the word used for a statue of a god (*statua* being used for the representation of a mortal). **fastigium**: A pediment, as of a temple, was added to Caesar's house in the forum. According to Suetonius (*Life of Julius Caesar*, 81.3) the night before his assassination his wife Calpurnia dreamt, among other things, that it collapsed. A **flamen** was a priest within the college of *pontifices* assigned to a particular god. There were 12 minor *flamines* and three *flamines maiores* (see Livy i.20.2), whom Cicero proceeds to itemise.

est ergo flamen... divo Iulio M. Antonius: 'There is a priest... (dedicated to) the deified Julius Caesar, (namely) Mark Antony'. Cicero, if he had lived, would have had to swallow his own sarcasm. This is the first use of the phrase **divus Iulius**, which later became standard for a deified emperor. Although Caesar was preparing the way for his own deification (or so the honours he sought imply), he only achieved it after his death, probably in the first year of the Triumvirate (42 BC). The deification itself is commemorated by an inscription (ILS 72). And Antony did become *flamen divi Iulii* in 40 BC (Plutarch, *Antony* 33.1).

cur non inaugureris?: The installation of a priest took place at an assembly called the *comitia celata*, in the presence of the pontiffs and officiated over by an augur (see notes on §§ 80-81 – Cicero was one, as was Antony; hence **conlegae sumus** in the next sentence).

vide qui te inauguret: **vide** = *quaere*. **qui** for *eum qui*, incorporation of the antecedent into the relative clause **NLG 251.1** – as we do in English: 'See who might install you.' **inauguret** is subjunctive of purpose **NLG 282.2**.

o detestabilem hominem: Accusative of exclamation **NLG 183**. **sive... sive...**: 'whether... or...'. Cicero is emphasising that priests are for gods, but Caesar was a tyrant and is a dead man: in neither capacity does he deserve a priest.

hodiernus dies: 19 September – see 'Introduction – Historical Background'. **qui sit**: *qui* interrogative adjective **NLG 90.2**.

quartum... diem ludorum Romanorum: The *ludi Romani* were one of the great public festivals at Rome, spanning 4–18 September [Ramsey]. Such *ludi publici* comprised different events, including chariot races in the circus – there were four *dies in circo* for the *ludi Romani*, as well as athletic contests and displays, and four days of theatrical performances (*ludi scenici*).

te... ad populum tulisse ut...: 'You brought (the proposal) before the people that...'; Antony's proposal, that a fifth day be added to the **ludi Romani** in honour of Caesar, would have been made at a legislative assembly. A different proposal of Antony's, that an extra day be added to all public thanksgivings (**supplicationes**) in Caesar's honour was passed by the senate on 1 September (*Philippic* 1.13) in Cicero's absence and is mentioned below (**an supplicationes...**). Antony refrained from observing the 19 September extension to the **ludi Romani** and thus is taunted by Cicero. It was eventually added under Augustus.

praetextati: Wearing the *toga praetexta* (see § 44 note), the badge of curule magistrates and priests, seems, from this passage, to have been de rigueur at public festivals.

tua lege: 'Your' law because moved by Antony.

an supplicationes... noluisti?: The two halves of the sentence are in parataxis, i.e. the first (**supplicationes... passus es**) is parallel to the second (**pulvinaria... noluisti**) and not joined to it, when we would expect it to begin with a conjunction like 'although'. The parataxis makes for a strong *antithesis. **supplicationes... contaminari** – by adding a day in honour of a dead man to celebrations giving thanks to the gods. **pulvinaria**: sc. *contaminari* with **noluit**. Cicero speaks as if the *pulvinaria*, which were an integral part of celebrating **supplicationes** (see note above on **pulvinar**), were not also part of the whole **ludi Romani**. The easiest explanation is that Antony did not permit Caesar's **pulvinaria** to appear at either **supplicationes** or **ludi Romani**.

usque quaque – 'completely'.

Section 111

quaeris placeatne mihi...: For **quaeris num placeat....** NLG 300.1.b; **mihi** with **placeat**. Cicero pre-empts the objection that he cannot criticise Antony for not endorsing some honours to Caesar when he himself is opposed to all of them: he at least is consistent.

acta Caesaris: See note on § 100, **acta enim Caesaris**. **quid potes dicere cur... cures?**: 'What can you say as to why...?'

nisi forte vis fateri: vis from *volo*.

quaestu... dignitate...: These are ablatives of means **NLG 218** rather than measure (degree of difference) **NLG 223** with **metiri** – 'measure by your profit, not by his distinction'.

quid ad haec tandem?: sc. *respondebis*. The idea is picked up by **respondebisne ad haec** three sentences on. **tandem**, in questions; has the force of, 'I ask you'.

...eloquentiam. disertissimum...: **disertus** is 'articulate', a degree lower than *eloquens*, 'eloquent'; in his *De Oratore*, Cicero cites his own remark that he had encountered several **disertos**, but nobody *eloquens*, 'who could in a more admirable and noble manner amplify and adorn whatever subjects he chose, and who embraced in thought and memory all the principles of everything relating to oratory' [i.94, translation J.S. Watson]. Hence **apertiorem**, 'more unbuttoned' –

though this is a *double entendre*, as we soon find with **nudus** in the next sentence. **avum tuum**: M. Antonius, consul in 99 BC, was one of the most celebrated orators of his day and is given a prominent role in Cicero's *De Oratore*.

ille numquam nudus: Cicero is referring to Antony's addressing the crowd in the Forum at the Lupercalia on 15 February, clad as Lupercus only in a goatskin (see note on § 84, **Lupercalia**). **tuum hominis simplicis pectus: hominis simplicis** is in apposition to the genitive implicit in **tuum** – 'your breast, that of an uncomplicated chap'.

aut omnino hiscere audebis?: 'or will you dare to open your mouth at all?'. This is the only occurrence of **hisco** in Cicero, but it is always derogatory.

ecquid... cui te respondere posse confidas: The construction changes from **respondeo** + acc to **respondeo** + dat (**cui** is neuter, referring to *ecquid*). The subjunctive in **confidas** is generic **NLG 283**.

Section 112

sed praeterita omittamus: Hortatory/jussive subjunctive **NLG 274**. Having trawled through the past in detail, Cicero can only use **omittamus** in the sense of 'turn from' (rather than 'leave out').

hunc unum diem... defende: i.e. defend your conduct today.

cur armatorum corona...: Another mention of Antony's troop of bodyguards (see note on § 46 **cum... meminisses**, and on § 104 **remove... quos videmus**). The word **corona** was used to describe any ring of bystanders, for example at a speech. Cicero's readers can gather from his repeated mention of Antony's retinue, here with detail of naked weapons (**gladiis... sagittis...**), that there were potent reasons why this speech was not delivered (see 'Introduction – Historical Background'). Here and in the forthcoming peroration (§ 116), weapons are scorned as false security. **cur valvae Concordiae non patent?**: sc. *templi* with **Concordiae**. This is where the senate had met; except for emergencies (and Antony may have contended that this occasion was one) the doors (here **valvae**) of the senate chamber would be open to allow the public to hear the debate; instead Antony had made the temple a prison, as Cicero observed in *Philippic* 5.18.

maxime barbaros: **maxime** is added to make up for the non-existent superlative of **barbarus**; the *hyperbole ('the most savage of any race') does not bear inspection. For these Ituraean archers, whose arrows (**sagittis**) are not so much their badge as the visible sign of their readiness, see note on § 108 **barbaria**.

praesidi sui causa: 'for his own protection', **praesidi** for *praesidii*, **NLG 25.2**; **sui** as if objective genitive **NLG 200**. **dicit**: It is unlikely (despite Appian (*Civil Wars*, iii.4)) that the senate itself voted Antony this bodyguard – Cicero would not then have been able to inveigh against it so whole-heartedly.

non = *nonne*. **miliens perire**: 'To die a thousand times' - a regular hyperbole. **in sua civitate**: 'In one's own state'.

Section 113

eripiet... tibi ista...: With **ista** supply *arma*. **tibi** = 'from you', the dative as normal after verbs of depriving **NLG 188.2.d**. **utinam salvis nobis!**: The ablative absolute **NLG 227.1** is unusual after **utinam**, but clear – 'May we live to see it!' [McElduff].

egeris... potes: After the future perfect (**egeris**) the future (*poteris*) might be expected – **non potes** in the present makes the impossibility more immediate. **uteris** could be present or future, but more probably present, again, for immediacy. **istis consiliis** – of armed menace.

tua minime avara coniunx: This is acerbic – elsewhere Cicero describes Fulvia, Antony's wife, as *mulier avarissima* (*Philippic* 6.4); *non solum avarissima sed etiam crudelissima uxor* (*Philippic* 13.18). Already in this speech she has featured as the merchant of fake Caesarian decrees (§ 95). Cicero here describes her as generous because she has 'already parted with two husbands' [King] – P. Clodius had been killed in Rome (52 BC – see §§ 21–22), C. Curio while leading an invasion of Africa on Caesar's behalf (in 49 BC). **quam sine contumelia describo**: 'whom I describe without malice', i.e. as **minime avara**. The malice is not only towards Fulvia but but also towards Antony, the **tertiam pensionem** (third instalment; **pensio** is often used of a debt repayment): it is he whom she 'owes' to the Roman people and should not hang on to jealously.

habet populus Romanus ad quos gubernacula rei publicae deferat: **ad quos** refers to the conspirators, especially those in senior magistracies – the praetors M. Brutus and C. Cassius, and D. Brutus the governor of Cisalpine Gaul. **gubernacula** – the 'ship of state' metaphor was so well worn that the word 'helm' (here, as regularly, in the plural) would be automatically understood as 'government' (of which it is the etymological root cf. § 92). **deferat** is generic subjunctive **NLG 283.1**.

ubicumque terrarum: 'Wherever in the world', partitive genitive (or genitive of the whole **NLG 201.3**). Cicero wrote to Atticus on 25 October 44 BC, 'Of Brutus you say you know nothing' (*ad Att.* 15.13.4); but he was in contact with Cassius, who received a copy of *Philippic I* in September (*ad Fam.* 12.2.1). What matters here, however, is the rhetorical point that the Republic is wherever they may happen to be. Cicero had written to Cassius on 3 May, 'Believe me, Cassius, I never cease thinking about you and our dear Brutus, that is, about the entire Republic, all hope for which depends on you two and Decimus Brutus.' [*ad Fam.* 12.1.1] Later in the same letter he continues, as if in rehearsal for this speech: 'Up to the present <the Republic> has avenged its injuries by the death of the tyrant through your hands: nothing more. Which of its dignities has it recovered? Is it that it now obeys the man in his grave whom it could not endure in his life-time? Do we support the rough drafts of a man [i.e. Antony], whose laws we ought to have torn down from the walls?' [*ad Fam.* 12.1.2] **se... ulta est, nondum recuperavit**: **se** is the object of both verbs. As the passage from the letter shows, **recuperavit** refers primarily to the Republic's *modus operandi*.

adulescentes nobilissimos paratos defensores: **adulescens** is Cicero's normal word for 'young man' (rather than *iuvenis*). It usually denotes 17–30 year-olds, but here describes Brutus and Cassius, who were in their 40s. **paratos defensores** – 'prepared as defenders', i.e. prepared to defend it.

quam volent illi cedant otio consulentes: 'Let them retreat as much as they (will) wish in the interests of peace'. **cedant** is jussive **NLG 275**. Cicero quotes Brutus's motive in leaving Italy as being to avoid provoking civil war [*Philippic* 10.8]. **tamen** first word after the concessive **quam ... consulentes** (see note on § 47 **tamen**).

et nomen... interest: Cicero is warning that peace cannot be achieved by accepting servitude.

non modo bello sed morte etiam: **bello** and **morte** are either ablatives of instrument **NLG 218**, 'by war... by death'; or ablatives of price **NLG 225**, 'at the price of war... of death'.

Section 114

e conspectus nostro: See note on § 113. **ubicumque terrarum** for the absence of the liberators. **at** = 'at least', common after a (virtually) negative conditional.

Tarquinium Brutus: See note on § 87 **L. Tarquinius. cum Romae esse licebat: esse** for *(regem) esse*. **Romae** is locative **NLG 21.2.c**. The indicative after **cum** indicates a point in time, 'at a period when' **NLG 288.1.A**.

Sp. Cassius, Sp. Maelius, M. Manlius: See note on all these in § 87. **suspicionem regni appetendi**: 'Suspicion of seeking kingship'. **hi primum...**: 'Caesar's assassins for the first time...' **in regnum appetentem: in** with **appetentem**, whose object is **regnum**.

quod cum ipsum factum... tum... praesertim cum...: quod... ipsum factum, connecting relative **NLG 251.6**, 'This very deed....' The first **cum** goes with the **tum**; together they mean 'both... and....' **praesertim cum** = 'especially since', causal **NLG 286.2. caelo capi** = 'to be contained by the heavens'. Cicero is plainly insinuating that Caesar's assassins have provided an example for others to follow on Antony. **satis... fructus: fructus** is partitive genitive (genitive of the whole) after **satis NLG 201.2**. The order in which to take the sentence is *Etsi enim satis fructus erat in ipsa conscientia....* **mortali immortalitatem**: A sort of *figura etymologica which brings home the magnificence of the assassins' deed.

Section 115

§§ 115 – 119 – CONCLUSIO/PERORATIO: The final appeal to Antony to renounce tyranny.

recordare igitur: *recordare* is imperative from *recordor*. **igitur** because the glory of removing a tyranny, just described, is greater than that of establishing one's own. **quo dictaturam sustulisti:** See § 91 and notes, where Cicero lauds Antony for achieving the abolition of the title of dictator (**dictaturae nomen in perpetuum de re publica sustulisti**). He had already made much of this action of Antony in *Philippic I* (§§ 3, 32), in the second of whose passages he also speaks of the joy of the people (knowing Antony cultivated popular opinion).

confer. . .: sc. *haec*, i.e. your previous good action and the reaction to it. **nundinatione:** Market-day trading – the word is pejorative even by commercial standards see note on § 92. Cicero is harking back to the trade in **acta Caesaris** (§ 100).

tum: i.e. if you make the comparison just mentioned. **laudem et lucrum:** 'praise and profit', Ramsey suggests, to preserve the *alliteration.

sed nimirum, ut. . . sic. . .: The **ut** and **sic** are correlatives – 'just as. . ., so. . .'. **quidam** is plural. **morbo aliquo et sensus stupore:** Ablative of cause **NLG 219**. The two phrases are linked – 'the dulling of the senses (brought on) by some disease', i.e. a *hendiadys. By this Cicero isolates the **stupor**, which is the impression of Antony he most wants to communicate (Cicero accuses Antony of it in two other places in this speech, as he does of being *sine sensu*).

iudicia non metuis: Antony as consul and afterwards as proconsul (for five years) had immunity from prosecution.

propter vim: 'on account of the violence (you make use of)'. **qui. . . ei. . .:** Correlative – 'he who. . . (what should) that man (fear?)'; **ei** is dative with the gerundive of obligation **NLG 189.1. timeat:** Generic subjunctive **NLG 283. isto modo:** 'after your fashion'.

Section 116

quod a corpore tuo prohibentur armis: **quod** is causal. The subject here are the **viri fortes egregiique cives**, the **armis** those of Antony's bodyguard.

timere a suis: 'To fear (danger) from one's own men' – **timere** is here intransitive, i.e. without an object. **dies et noctes** are accusatives of duration of time **NLG 181.1**. Cicero muses on the tyrant's terror at some length in *de Officiis* 2.23–26, citing the examples of Dionysius and Phalaris. Caesar had attempted to face it down, dismissing his bodyguard a few months before he was murdered and, according to Plutarch, 'saying that it was better to die once for all than to be always expecting death' (*Caesar*, 57.4). Plutarch goes on to mention Caesar's grain distributions/allowances and banquets, which Cicero also mentions at the end of the chapter (**congiariis, epulis**), as an alternative means of self-preservation.

nisi vero...: The idea is implicit, '(And that will be exactly your position) unless...'. **maioribus... beneficiis**: Ablative of instrument **NLG 218**. **quam ille quosdam habuit ex eis a quibus est interfectus**: '(Unless you have men bound to you by greater favours) than (those by which) he (Caesar) had (bound to him, sc. **obligatos**) certain of those by whom he was killed'. The point is that Antony would have to outdo Caesar in largesse towards **all** his followers to buy their loyalty. The plunder from Caesar's campaigns in Gaul enabled him to bankroll support among the senate and elsewhere (Suetonius, *Life of Julius Caesar*, 27; Dio Cassius 44.39.3–5). Even Cicero owed Caesar money at this time (50 BC – *ad Att*. 7.8.5). More significantly, perhaps, many of Caesar's assassins were viewed as 'friends' – Seneca (*de Ira*, 3.30.4) says that more friends than enemies killed him, out of disappointed hopes. **aut ulla re**: The first **aut** dismisses the possibility that Antony could have elicited the same loyalty as Caesar by generosity; this second **aut** is a catch-all: there is in fact no characteristic of Caesar in which Antony surpasses him and to which he might look for his salvation. **ulla re** is ablative of respect **NLG 226** – 'in anything'.

ingenium... diligentia: This perhaps unexpected tribute to Caesar's talents is consistent with Cicero's comments elsewhere. He describes Caesar's *vis ingenii* as *summa* (*Philippics* 5.49); his *memoria* is a quality in which he excels (*qua vales plurimum* – *pro Deiotaro* 49); in oratory, he yields to nobody (*Brutus* 261) and his commentaries (i.e. Gallic Wars) are *valde probandos* (*Brutus* 262). **diligentia** Cicero defines (*de Oratore* 2.149) as comprising **cura** and **cogitatio**; it is not, however, an undisputed virtue of Caesar's – the historian Asinius Pollio said the commentaries were *parum diligenter compositos* ('written with too little precision') (Suetonius, *Life of Julius Caesar* 56.4).

at tamen magnas: 'But great all the same'. **at tamen** is in very strong opposition to **quamvis**.

multos annos regnare meditatus: The point at which Caesar conceived his desire for dictatorship is debatable – Suetonius (*Life of Julius Caesar* 30.5, quoting Cicero's *de Officiis*), claims Caesar had set his heart on it from early youth (*prima aetate*), but this could easily be the interpretation of hindsight. **cogitarat** for *cogitaverat* **NLG 116.1**.

muneribus... epulis: Ablatives of instrument **NLG 218. muneribus** – Caesar decreed extravagant gladiatorial games in honour of his father (65 BC) and of his daughter (46 BC) – she had died eight years before. **monumentis** – Caesar began constructing in central Rome, again with spoils from his wars in Gaul, the Basilica Iulia and Forum Iulium; in 54 BC Cicero had assisted in purchasing the land for these projects (*ad Att.* 4.17.7); Augustus completed them (*Res Gestae* 20).

Caesar is also said to have enlarged the Circus Maximus (Pliny, *Natural History* 36.(24).102). **congiariis** – from the liquid measure *congius*, about six pints, used for grain; but the **congiarium** could also be a cash handout. Cicero may be referring here to Caesar's distribution after his series of four triumphs in 46 BC (Suetonius, *Life of Julius Caesar* 38.1); this was a mixture of grain, oil and money. **epulis** –after the triumphs of 46, Caesar provided lavish banquets ('feasting them all at one time on 20,000 couches' – Plutarch, *Caesar* 55.4). In 45 BC, after defeating Pompey's sons in Spain, he gave two more banquets (Suetonius, *Life of Julius Caesar* 38.2).

suos praemiis: Caesar was famously generous to his friends (Suetonius, *Life of Julius Caesar* 72); Cicero observes that sometimes these 'benefactions' were concessions won from him (*ad Fam.* 12.18.2). **praemiis** is ablative of instrument, as is **specie NLG 218**.

adversarios clementiae specie devinxerat: After Pharsalus in 48 BC, Caesar notably spared M. Brutus and C. Cassius (his future assassins) and allowed them to advance their careers within his regime. **specie** and **devinxerat** ('chained') cast a negative light on Caesar's mercy, as if it was for show and out of self-interest only. Cicero's compliments towards Caesar's mercy elsewhere are more wholehearted, in his speeches but more significantly in his letters (e.g. *ad Fam.* 6.10b); even so, as Ramsey comments, the sense that mercy could only be dispensed by a superior was a worry: Cassius, in a letter to Cicero (*ad Fam.* 15.19.4) calls Caesar his *veterem et clementem* **dominum**. Cicero quotes his friend Curio's warning, 'that Caesar himself was not by taste or nature averse from bloodshed, but thought clemency would win him popularity: if, however, he once lost the affection of the people, he would be cruel'. [*ad Att.* 10.4.8, in 48 BC; Perseus translation].

quid multa?: 'Why should I say more'?

liberae civitati: With **attulerat** – 'he brought to a free state....'. **partim metu partim patientia**: **metu** and **patientia** are ablatives of cause **NLG 219** 'partly through its timidity, partly through its acquiescence'. Plutarch (*Caesar* 57.1) says the Roman people accepted 'the bit' (like a horse), treating Caesar's dominion as relief from civil war – and therefore appointed him dictator for life.

Section 117

cum illo... te... conferre possum: 'I can compare you with him (Caesar)'. **dominandi cupiditate**: Ablative of respect – as **ceteris rebus NLG 226**. **nullo modo**: Ablative of manner **NLG 220** – 'in no way'.

inusta: A metaphor, branding indelibly, that Cicero liked using but almost exclusively in his speeches – it has shock-value.

hoc... boni est quod...: **boni** is partitive genitive **NLG 201.2** – **hoc boni est** = 'this is the good result'; **quod...** = 'that...' **NLG 299.1.a**. The message is that Romans have learnt not to trust someone with monarchical pretensions – such as Antony clearly nurtures. **quantum cuique crederet**: Lit. 'how much to should trust each person', i.e. 'how much to trust anyone'. **a quibus caveret**: 'From whom they should watch out (for trouble)'. Cf. **timere a suis** in § 116.

quam sit... occidere?: The **quam** ('how...') goes with each adjective (**pulchrum... gratum... gloriosum**) and introduces an indirect question (hence the subjunctive **sit**) **NLG 300.1**. **re pulchrum**: **re** is most naturally taken as an ablative of respect **NLG 226; beneficio** and **fama** are ablatives of cause **NLG 219**.

an...: This can introduce an additional question **NLG 162.4.a**, like 'or...' in English.

Section 118

ad hoc opus curretur: curretur is impersonal passive, 'men will run' NLG 256.3. **occasionis tarditas**: A condensed phrase, for 'slowness in (seizing) the opportunity'.

respice... considera: This is parataxis, the two halves of the sentence in *asyndeton dividing at **M. Antoni**. The indirect questions beginning **quibus...** and **non quibuscum...** are governed by **considera**. **aliquando** = 'at last' (as later in this same chapter). **quibus ortus sis**: With **orior**, the construction is normally with *e(x)/a(b)* before the ablative, but these can be omitted even in classical authors. Cicero is more specific about which forebears in *Philippic* 1.27, where he says Antony might imitate the consulships of his grandfathers (M. Antonius, consul in 99 BC; L. Iulius Caesar, consul in 90 BC) and uncle (another L. Iulius Caesar, consul in 64 BC). **non quibuscum vivas**: i.e. Fulvia, Antony's wife, and his brother Lucius, who at this time was a tribune, sitting as chairman on a recently established agrarian board (*Philippic* 5.7).

mecum, ut voles: sc. *fac* or similar. **ut voles** = 'as you (shall) want' – i.e. what matters is not your relationship with me, but your relationship with the Republic. **in gratiam**: 'into favour'.

videris: An unusual use of the future perfect indicative almost as a command – 'you will see about yourself'. Some treat it as perfect subjunctive.

adulescens: At the time of the Catilinarian conspiracy (63 BC) Cicero was 43. See note on § 113 **adulescentes nobilissimos paratos defensores**.

quin etiam corpus libenter obtulerim: quin etiam = 'Yes, and...'; the phrase in a negative context means 'Rather....'. **corpus** for 'life'. **obtulerim** is potential (perfect) subjunctive, 'I would offer...' NLG 280.2. **potest** is indicative to make the possibility of liberty returning more real and immediate.

Section 119

etenim...: Cicero continues contemplating his own death and his lack of reluctance. **abhinc annos prope viginti**: 'Almost twenty years ago'. The accusative of duration of time is used with **abhinc NLG 1981.1**. Again, Cicero is recalling the Catilinarian conspiracy, and in particular his Fourth Catilinarian, delivered in the Temple of Concord (**hoc ipso in templo**) on 5 December 63 BC. Cicero imagines delivering this speech in the same meeting place of the senate as on 19 September. (For its non-delivery, see 'Introduction – Historical Background'.) **quanto verius**: 'How much more truly...?' **quanto** is ablative of measure of difference **NLG 223**. **seni** balances **consulari** – sc. 'will I say that death comes not too soon for'. At the end of the First Philippic (1.38), Cicero had remarked that he had lived long enough for his own life-span and for his own distinction.

optanda mors est: In his letters since the early part of May (e.g. *ad Att.* 14.19.1) and in the recently written *de Senectute* (end of 19), Cicero had been speaking of death as the port reached after a long voyage. **perfuncto** agrees with **mihi**: 'Now I have carried out fully...'. There is some doubt about the text here, but as it stands the two relative clauses constitute a *zeugma with **rebus – rebus quas adeptus sum** means 'the political offices which I obtained', while **rebus quas gessi** means 'the deeds which I achieved'.

duo modo haec opto...: As if dismissing the choice for himself in the previous sentence, in this last sentence Cicero states his two public wishes, **unum ut..., alterum ut....** This **ut/ne** construction is normal after verbs of wishing **NLG 296**. Cicero's second wish – that each be rewarded in accordance to his service to the Republic – is both a declaration of his own clear conscience and a final spur to Antony.

Vocabulary

a, ab + *abl*	from, by
abduco, abducere, abduxi, abductum	I lead away, remove
abeo, abire, abi(v)I, abitum	I go away
abhinc	ago
abicio, abicere, abieci, abiectum	I discard
abiectus -a -um	deferential
abscondo, abscondere, abscondidi, absconditum	I hide, conceal
abstergeo, abstergere, abstersi, abstersum	I wipe off
absum, abesse, afui	I am absent, am away, am distant
ac, atque	and
accedo, accedere, accessi, accessum	I come up to
accipio, accipere, accepi, acceptum	I accept, take in, receive, hear
actum -i, n	deed; transaction
ad + *acc*	to, towards, at, about, near
addo, addere, addidi, additum	I add, join
adfero, adferre, attuli, adlatum	I bring
adhortor, adhortari, adhortatus sum	I urge
adhuc	till now, still
adipiscor, adipisci, adeptus sum	I obtain
aditus, aditus, m	entrance

adlicio, adlicere, adlexi, adlectum	I attract
admitto, admittere, admisi, admissum	I permit; commit (*often in phrase 'in se admittere'*)
adopto, adoptare, adoptavi, adoptatum	I choose, adopt
adrogantia -ae, f	arrogance
adsoleo, adsolere	I am accustomed (only used impersonally)
adulescens, adulescentis, m	youth, young man
adversarius -a -um	opposing
advolo, advolare, advolavi, advolatum	I fly to
aedes, aedis, f	temple
aes alienum, n	debt
aes, aeris, n	bronze; money
ager, agri, m	field, land, territory
agmen, agminis, n	column of men, army
Agnaninus -a -um	of Agnania
ago, agere, egi, actum	I do, act, drive, discuss
alienus -a -um	belonging to another
alii ... alii	some ... others
aliquando	some day, at some point; at last, finally
aliquis, aliquid	someone, something, anyone, anything
alius, alia, aliud	other; one... another; else
alter, altera, alterum	the other, one (of two), another, a second
amicio, amicire, amicui/amixi, amictum	I wrap round
amicus -i, m	friend

amo, amare, amavi, amatum	I love, like
amor, amoris, m	love
an	or (in questions)
animus -i, m	spirit, soul, mind, courage
annus -i, m	year
ante + *acc*	before, in front of; (*as adv*) previously
antea	before, previously
aperio, aperire, aperui, apertum	I open, reveal, disclose
apparatus, apparatus, m	(magnificent) preparation
appareo, apparere, apparui, apparitum	I appear
apparitor, apparitoris, m	functionary, servant
appeto, appetere, appeti(v)I, appetitum	I seek after
approbo, approbare, approbavi, approbatum	I approve, support
Aprilis -e	of April
Aquinas, Aquinatis, c	inhabitant of Aquinum
aratio, arationis, f	public plot of arable land
aratrum -i, n	plough
arbitror, arbitrari, arbitratus sum	I think, consider
arceo, arcere, arcui, arctum	I debar, keep at a distance
ardeo, ardere, arsi, arsum	I burn, blaze
arma, armorum, n pl	arms, weapons, armour
armo, armare, armavi, armatum	I arm
ascribo, ascribere, ascripsi, ascriptum + *acc* + *dat*	I attribute, ascribe; inscribe; add

assevero, asseverare, asseveravi, asseveratum	I declare
at	but
atque	and
attentus -a -um	attentive
auctor, auctoris, m	creator
audacia -ae, f	boldness, impudence
audax, audacis	bold, daring
audeo, audere, ausus sum	I dare
audio, audire, audivi, auditum	I hear, listen to
aufero, auferre, abstuli, ablatum	I take away, carry off, steal
augur, auguris, m	augur
aureus -a -um	golden
auspicato	having taken the auspices
auspicium -i, n	omen, augury
auspicor, auspicari,, auspicatus sum	I take the auspices
aut	or, either
autem	but, however
avarus -a -um	mean
aversus -a -um	turned away; from the back
avoco, avocare, avocavi, avocatum	I deter
avus -i, m	grandfather
barbaria -ae, f	barbarity
barbarus -a -um	foreign, barbarian
bellum -i, n	war
beneficium -i, n	kindness, service, favour
benevolentia -ae, f	goodwill
bibo, bibere, bibi	I drink
bonus -a -um	good

bustum -i, n	tomb
caelum -i, n	sky, heaven
calamitas, calamitatis, f	disaster
calamitosus -a -um	calamitous
Campanus -a -um	of Campania
campus -i, m	plain, field
capio, capere, cepi, captum	I take, catch, capture; contain
Capitolium -i, n	Capitol
capto, captare, captavi, captatum	I court, seek
caput, capitis, n	head, person, life, capital
caritas, caritatis, f	affection
Casinas, Casinatis	of Casinum
causa -ae, f	cause, reason, case
gen + **causa**	for the sake of
caveo, cavere, cavi, cautum	I beware (of), take care
cedo, cedere, cessi, cessum	I yield, give up; (in compounds) go
celer, celeris, celere	quick
certatim	with competition, in rivalry
certus -a -um	certain, sure, fixed
cesso, cessare, cessavi, cessatum	I delay, tarry
ceteri -ae -a	the rest, the other
chirographum -i, n	hand-written document
cibus -i, m	food
circumduco, circumducere, circumduxi, circumductum	I lead, haul round
circus -i, m	circus, arena
cito (*comp* **citius**)	rapidly
civilis -e	civil
civis, civis, m/f	citizen
civitas, civitatis, f	citizenship, state, city, tribe

clam	secretly
classis, classis, f	(census) class
clementia -ae, f	mercy
cliens, clientis, m	client, dependent
cogitatio, cogitationis, f	thought(fulness), reflection
cogito, cogitare, cogitavi, cogitatum	I think, consider
cognitio, cognitionis, f	knowledge, investigation
cognosco, cognoscere, cognovi, cognitum	I get to know, find out, learn, investigate
cogo, cogere, coegi, coactum	I force, compel, drive, assemble
cohortatio, cohortationis, f	incitement, call to action
colo, colere, colui, cultum	I cultivate, worship, honour
colonia -ae, f	colony
colonus -i, m	colonist
comitia – orum, n pl	electoral assembly
commemoro, commemorare, commemoravi, commemoratum	I mention, enumerate
commendo, commendare, commendavi, commendatum	I entrust, commit; recommend; announce support for someone as candidate
committo, committere, commisi, commissum	I commit, fight, begin (battle)
commoveo, commovere, commovi, commotum	I upset
comparo, comparare, comparavi, comparatum	I prepare, provide, obtain, compare
compransor, compransoris, m	fellow feaster
concedo, concedere, concessi, concessum	I grant, concede

concido, concidere, concidi	I collapse
concutio, concutere, concussi, concussum	I shake, damage
confero, conferre, contuli, conlatum	I collect, compare, contribute, bestow
conficio, conficere, confeci, confectum	I complete, wear out
confidentia -ae, f	confidence, audacity
confido, confidere, confisus sum + *dat*	I trust, believe, have confidence (in)
confirmo, confirmare, confirmavi, confirmatum	I give assurance that, confirm
confiteor, confiteri, confessus sum	I confess
congiarium -i, n	gift
congressio, congressionis, f	association
coniunx, coniugis, m/f	husband, wife, spouse
conlega -ae, m	colleague
conlegium -i, n	college
conloco, conlocare, conlocavi, conlocatum	I establish
conlusor, conlusoris, m	fellow gambler
conor, conari, conatus sum + *inf*	I try
conscientia -ae, f	consciousness, conscience
conscribo, conscribere, conscripsi, conscriptum	I enroll (*and see* patres conscripti)
consequor, consequi, consecutus sum	I obtain
conservo, conservare, conservavi, conservatum	I save, protect
considero, considerare, consideravi, consideratum	I consider

consilium -i, n	plan, advice, prudence; council, committee
consisto, consistere, constiti, constitum	I halt, stand, stand firm
conspectus, conspectus, m	sight
constituo, constituere, constitui, constitutum	I decide, establish
consto, constare, constiti, constatum	I agree
consuetudo, consuetudinis, f	familiarity, custom
consul, consulis, m	consul
consularis, consularis, m	consular, ex-consul
consulatus consulatus, m	consulship
consulo, consulere, consului, consultum	I consult, consider, advise; (+ *dat*) consult the interests of
consultum -i, n	decree (of senate)
contamino, contaminare, contaminavi, contaminatum	I pollute
contemno, contemnere, contempsi, contemptum	I scorn, disparage
continuo	immediately, directly
contionor, contionari, contionatus sum	I deliver a speech
contra + *acc*	against
contumelia -ae, f	insult
convello, convellere, convulsi, convulsum	I undermine, nullify
convoco, convocare, convocavi, convocatum	I call together
copiosus -a -um	eloquent
corona -ae, f	crown, ring

corono, coronare, coronavi, coronatum	I crown
corpus, corporis, n	body
cotidie	every day, daily
credo, credere, credidi, creditum + *dat*	I believe, trust, entrust
creo, creare, creavi, creatum	I elect
cruento, cruentare, cruentavi, cruentatum	I stain with blood
culpa, culpae, f	fault, blame
cum + *abl*	with
cum + *subj*	when, since, although
cum... tum...	both... and ...
cupiditas, cupiditatis, f	desire
cupio, cupere, cupivi, cupitum	I desire, wish, want
cur?	why?
cura -ae, f	care, charge, anxiety
curo, curare, curavi, curatum	I care for, cure; (*with gerundive*) get something done
curro, currere, cucurri, cursum	I run
cursus, cursus, m	course
custos, custodis, m/f	guard
de + *abl*	about, from, down from
debeo, debere, debui, debitum	I owe; (+ *inf*) ought
decet + *acc* + *inf*	it is fitting for X to
decoctor, decoctoris, m	bankrupt, ruined man
decoquo, decoquere, decoxi, decoctum	I boil away; go bankrupt
deduco, deducere, deduxi, deductum	I lead away, lead to a particular place; found (colony)

defendo, defendere, defendi, defensum	I defend
defensio, defensionis, f	defence
defensor, defensoris, m	defender
defero, deferre, detuli, delatum	I confer, deliver; refer, indict
deflagro, deflagrare, deflagravi, deflagratum	I burn down
deinceps	in turn
deinde, dein	then, next, afterwards
delenio, delenire, deleni(v)I, delenitum	I soften, win over, allure
deminuo, deminuere, deminui, deminutum	I reduce, diminish
demiror, demirari, demiratus sum	I wonder (at)
demitto, demittere, demisi, demissum	I let down, lower
deporto, deportare, deportavi, deportatum	I carry off
descendo, descendere, descendi, descensum	I descend, come down
desero, deserere, deserui, desertum	I desert
desiderium -i, n	longing, sense of loss
desidero, desiderare, desideravi, desideratum	I long for, miss
desino, desinere, desii, desitum + *inf*	I cease
desperatio, desperationis, f	despair
detestabilis -e	hateful
detraho, detrahere, detraxi, detractum	I remove; drag down

detrimentum -i, n	loss
deus -i, m	god
deversorium -i, n	lodging
devincio, devincire, devinxi, devinctum	I bind fast
devius -a -um	off the road
diadema, diadematis, n	royal headband
dico, dicere, dixi, dictum	I say, speak, tell
dictator, dictatoris, m	dictator
dictatura -ae, f	dictatorship
dies, diei, m, *occasionally* f	day
diffugio, diffugere, diffugi	I scatter
dignitas, dignitatis, f	rank, dignity, importance, honour
dignus -a -um + *abl*	worthy (of), deserving (of)
diligens, diligentis	careful, diligent
diligentia -ae, f	thoroughness
discedo, discedere, discessi	I depart, leave
discessus, discessus, m	departure
discidium -i, n	separation, parting
disco, discere, didici	I learn
disertus -a -um	articulate
dispar, disparis	different
dissentio, dissentire, dissensi, dissensum	I disagree
dissimilis -e	different
dissimulo, dissimulare, dissimulavi, dissimulatum	I dissemble, hide
dissolvo, dissolvere, dissolvi, dissolutum	I pay, discharge
diu (*comparative* diutius)	for a long time
diuturnus -a -um	long-lasting

divido, dividere, divisi, divisum	I divide up, distribute
divino, divinare, divinavi, divinatum	I prophesy
divinus -a -um	godlike, divine
divus -a -um	deified, divine
do, dare, dedi, datum	I give
doctrina -ae, f	learning
dolor, doloris, m	pain, sorrow, anger
domesticus -a -um	private
dominatus, dominatus, m	domination
domino, dominare, dominavi, dominatum	I am master
dominus -i, m	master
domus, domus, f (*abl* domo/domu)	house, home
duco, ducere, duxi, ductum	I lead, take; marry; consider
dulcis -e	sweet
dum	while, until, provided that
duo, duae, duo	two
dux, ducis, m	leader, general, ruler
e, ex + *abl*	from, out of; (in compounds) out
ebrius -a -um	drunk
ecce	behold
ecquis, ecquid	is there anyone who/anything which?
efficio, efficere, effeci, effectum	I carry out, accomplish
effundo, effundere, effudi, effusum	I pour forth, squander
egeo, egere, egui + *gen or abl*	I need, am in want of, lack
egestas, egestatis, f	penury
ego, mei	I, me

egregius -a -um	exceptional, outstanding
eicio, eicere, eieci, eiectum	I throw out
elatus -a -um	lofty
eloquentia -ae, f	eloquence
eludo, eludere, elusi, elusum	I cheat
ementior, ementiri, ementitus sum	I fabricate, falsify (*ementitus* also as passive, 'falsified')
emo, emere, emi, emptum	I buy
enim	for
eo	thither
eo, ire, i(v)i	I go
epulae -arum, f	feasts
equidem	indeed, for my part
erga + *acc*	towards
ergo	therefore
eripio, eripere, eripui, ereptum	I snatch away
erumpo, erumpere, erupi, eruptum	I burst forth
escendo, escendere, escendi, escensum	I climb
et	and, (*et. . . et*) both. . . and
etenim	for truly; and indeed
etiam	also, even, still
etsi	although; and yet
evenio, evenire, eveni, eventum	I happen (*used impersonally*)
everto, evertere, everti, eversum	I destroy, overthrow
excito, excitare, excitavi, excitatum	I wake, rouse, excite
exemplum -i, n	example, precedent
exigo, exigere, exegi, exactum	I drive out
eximo, eximere, exemi, exemptum	I remove

existimo, existimare, existimavi, existimatum	I think
expilo, expilare, expilavi, expilatum	I pillage, plunder
expleo, explere, explevi, expletum	I fill to the brim, glut
expono, exponere, exposui, expositum	I put on show, display
exsilium -i, n	exile
exsisto, exsistere, exstiti, exstitum	I come forth, emerge
exspecto, exspectare, exspectavi, exspectatum	I wait for, expect
exsul, exsulis, m/f	exile
extorqueo, extorquere, extorsi, extortum	I wrench away
extremus -a -um	last, most recent
facilis -e	easy
facinerosus -a -um	criminal
facinus, facinoris, n	crime, outrage, deed
facio, facere, feci, factum (*in compounds* -ficio)	I make, do
facultas, facultatis, f	capacity, opportunity; (pl) resources
fallo, fallere, fefelli, falsum	I deceive, cheat
falsus -a -um	forged
fama -ae, f	rumour, fame, glory
familia -ae, f (*archaic gen sing* familias)	family, household
familiaris -e	of the family, close friend
familiaritas, familiaritatis, f	intimacy, friendship
fas n (*indeclinable*)	right

fasti -orum m pl	calendar showing festivals, events, magistrates
fastigium -i, n	pediment, as of temple
fateor, fateri, fassus sum	I acknowledge, confess
fax, facis, f	torch
fero, ferre, tuli, latum	I bear, carry, bring, say
festino, festinare, festinavi	I hurry
figo, figere, fixi, fixum	I fasten, attach
filius -i, m	son
fio, fieri, factus sum	I become, am made, happen
firmus -a -um	solid, dependable
flagitium -i, n	disgraceful act
flamen, flaminis, m	priest
florens, florentis	distinguished, of high repute
fodio, fodere, fodi, fossum	I dig; prick, wound
foedus -a -um	foul
foedus, foederis, n	treaty, agreement
formido, formidinis, f	fear
fortasse	perhaps
forte	by chance
fortis -e	brave, strong, bold
fortuna, fortunae, f	fate, luck, fortune (good or bad); (pl) wealth
forum -i, n	forum, market place
frequens, frequentis	populous
fructuosus -a -um	fruitful, profitable
fructus, fructus, m	fruit
frustra	in vain
fuga -ae, f	flight, escape
fuligo, fuliginis, f	soot
fundus -i, m	farm
funus, funeris, n	funeral

furiosus -a -um	wild
futurus -a -um (*fut part 'sum'*)	about to be, future
gemitus, gemitus, m	groan
gens, gentis, f	race, people, family, tribe, nation
gero, gerere, gessi, gestum	I bear, wear, wage war, manage, (with *res*) do
gladius -i, m	sword
gloria -ae, f	glory
gloriosus -a -um	glorious
grandifer, grandifera, grandiferum	productive
gratia -ae, f	favour, thanks, esteem
gratus -a -um	pleasing, welcome
gravis -e	heavy, serious, painful, important
gubernaculum -i, n	helm; (pl) government
guberno, gubernare, gubernavi, gubernatum	I steer (boat)
gustatus, gustatus, m	taste, appetite
habeo, habere, habui, habitum	I have, hold, consider
habito, habitare, habitavi, habitatum	I live, dwell
hasta -ae, f	spear; public auction
hercule	by Hercules
heres, heredis, m/f	heir
heri	yesterday
hic, haec, hoc	this
hisco, hiscere	I gape
hodie	today
hodiernus -a -um	of today
homo, hominis, m	man, person
honestus -a -um	decent, proper
honor/honos, honoris, m	honour, esteem, glory

hora -ae, f	hour
hortor, hortari, hortatus sum	I urge, encourage
hortus -i, m	garden
hospes, hospitis, m	guest, host
humilis -e	humble
iaceo, iacere, iacui	I lie (down)
iam	now, already
Ianuarius -a -um	of January
ibi	there, then
idem, eadem, idem	the same
ideo	on that account
Idus, Iduum, f	Ides, 13th of month (15th in March, May, July, October)
igitur	therefore, and so
ignoro, ignorare, ignoravi, ignoratum	I do not know, am ignorant, misunderstand
ille, illa, illud	that, he, she, it
illinc	from there
imitor, imitari, imitatus sum	I imitate
immaturus -a -um	premature, early
imminuo, imminuere, imminui, imminutum	I diminish
immitto, immittere, immisi, immissum	I send in
immortalis -e	immortal
immunitas, immunitatis, f	exemption from tax or public service
impedio, impedire, impedivi, impeditum	I delay, hinder, prevent, hamper
impello, impellere, impuli, impulsum	I urge on, encourage

imperitus -a -um	ignorant, inexperienced
imperium -i, n	command, power, empire
impero, imperare, imperavi, imperatum +*dat*	I order, command
impetus, impetus, m	attack, impulse
implico, implicare, implicavi, implicatum	I entwine, involve
impono, imponere, imposui, impositum	I place on
importunus -a -um	cruel, implacable
improbus -a -um	wicked
impudentia -e, f	shamelessness
impulsus, impulsus, m	pressure, instigation
in + *abl*	in, on
in + *acc*	into, onto, against, towards
inauguro, inaugurare, inauguravi, inauguratum	I install (with ceremony of augurs), inaugurate
incendium -i, n	fire
incendo, incendere, incendi, incensum	I burn, set on fire, inflame, rouse
incido, incidere, incidi	I fall upon, meet with
incido, incidere, incidi, incisum	I cut into, cut short
incolumis -e	intact, preserved
incredibilis -e	unbelievable
inde	from there, thereupon, next
indignus -a -um	unworthy
induco, inducere, induxi, inductum	I lead on; mislead
infimus -a -um	lowest
infligo, infligere, inflixi, inflictum	I inflict

ingenium, ingenii, n	character, ability
ingenuus -a -um	free-born
ingredior, ingredi, ingressus sum	I enter, undertake
inimicus -i, m	(personal) enemy
iniuria -ae, f	injustice, injury, wrong
innocentia -ae, f	innocence
innumerabilis -e	countless
inquam, inquit, inquiunt	I say
inquilinus -i, m	tenant, occupant
inscientia -ae, f	ignorance
insero, inserere, insevi, insitus	I insert, poke in
insignis, -e	distinguished, glorious
insolentia -ae, f	insolence
inspecto, inspectare, inspectavi, inspectatum	I look on, observe
inspicio, inspicere, inspexi, inspectum	I look at, inspect, examine
integer, integra, integrum	whole, irreproachable
intellego, intellegere, intellexi, intellectum	I understand, perceive, realise
inter + *acc*	between, among
intercedo, intercedere, intercessi, intercessum	I stand surety for (a certain amount)
interea, interim	meanwhile, in the meantime
interficio, interficere, interfeci, interfectum	I kill
interitus, interitus, m	demise
intersum, interesse, interfui	I lie between
intervenio, intervenire, interveni, interventum	I intervene, stand in the way of

interverto, intervertere, interverti, interversum	I divert, purloin,
intimus -a -um + *dat*	intimate with, close to
intro, intrare, intravi, intratum	I enter
inuro, inurere, inussi, inustum + *dat*	I brand on
invehor, invehi, invectus sum in + *acc*	I attack, inveigh against
invenio, invenire, inveni, inventum	I find, discover
inveteror, inveterari, inveteratus sum	I become established
invideo, invidere, invidi, invisum + *dat*	I hate
invitus -a -um	unwillling, reluctant
Iovi *see* Iuppiter	
ipse -a -um	-self
iratus -a -um	angry
irritus -a -um	null and void
is, ea, id	this, that, he, she, it
iste, ista, istud	that (person, thing) - *freq. derogatory*
ita	in this way, so, thus
itaque	and so, therefore
iter, itineris, n	journey, march, way
iudicium – i, n	court, judgement, discernment
iugerum -i, n (*gen pl* iugerum)	measure of land (2/3 acre)
Iunius -a -um	of June
Iuppiter, Iovis, m	Jupiter
ius, iuris, n	right, justice
iussus, iussus, m	order, command

Kalendae – arum, f pl	Calends, 1st of month
labor, laboris, m	work, toil, trouble
lacero, lacerare, laceravi, laceratum	I tear, to pieces, mutilate
lacrimo, lacrimare, lacrimavi, lacrimatum	I cry, weep, lament
laetitia -ae, f	joy
laetor, laetari, laetatus sum	I rejoice
largitio, largitionis, f	distribution, largesse
latro, latronis, m	robber
laudatio, laudationis, f	(speech of) praise
laudo, laudare, laudavi, laudatum	I praise
laus, laudis, f	praise, honour, credit
lectica -ae, f	litter
lectus -i, m	bed, couch
Leontinus -a -um	of Leontini (in Sicily)
lex, legis, f	law
libens, libentis	willing, glad
liber, libera, liberum	free
liberator, liberatoris, m	liberator
libero, liberare, liberavi, liberatum	I set free
libertas, libertatis, f	freedom
libidinosus -a -um	lustful
libido, libidinis, f	desire, lust
licet, licere, licuit + *dat*	it is allowed
limen, liminis, n	threshold
littera, litterae, f *(usually pl with sg meaning)*	letter, literature
locus, loci, m	place, position, situation, opportunity

longus -a -um	long, far
loquor, loqui, locutus sum	I speak, talk
lucrum -i, n	gain
ludo, ludere, lusi, lusum	I play, gamble
ludus -i, m	game; school
Lupercalia -ium/orum, n pl	Lupercalia, festival of Lycean Pan
Lupercus -i, m	priest of Lycean Pan
lux, lucis, f	light, daylight
madeo, madere, madui	I drip
maereo, maerere, maerui	I lament, grieve
magister, magistri, m	teacher, master
magistratus, magistratus, m	office, position, magistracy
magnus -a -um	big, large, great
maior, maius	greater
Maius -a -um	of May
maledictum -i, n	abuse, slander; curse
malo, malle, malui	I prefer
malus -a -um	evil, bad
mando, mandare, mandavi, mandatum	I commit, entrust, command
maneo, manere, mansi, mansum	I remain, stay
manus, manus, f	hand, band
Mars, Martis, m	Mars
Martius -a -um	of March
mater, matris, f	mother
matrimonium -i, n	marriage
maximus -a -um	greatest
mecum	with me
medicus -i, m	doctor
meditatus -a -um	premeditated

Vocabulary

meditor, meditari, meditatus sum + *inf*	I contemplate doing
medius -a -um	middle (of)
memini, meminisse	I remember
memoria -ae, f	memory
mens, mentis, f	mind, mentality
mensis, mensis, m	month
merces, mercedis, f	fee, pay
mereor, mereri, meritus sum	I deserve
meretricius -a -um	of a prostitute
meritorius -a -um	for hire
metior, metiri, mensus sum	I measure
metuo, metuere, metui, metutum	I fear
metus, metus, m	fear
meus -a -um	my
miles, militis, m	soldier
miliens	a thousand times
mille (*indec*), **milia** (*pl*)	thousand
mima -ae, f	mime actress
mimus -i, m	mime actor
mina -ae, f	threat
minimus -a -um	least
minitor, minitari, minitatus sum + *dat*	I threaten
minor -us	less
minuo, minuere, minui, minutum	I diminish
minus	not (after *si*)
mirabilis -e	strange, wonderful
Misenus -a -um	at Misenum
miser, misera, miserum	miserable, wretched, sad

miseratio, miserationis, f	lament
miseret, miserere, miseruit + *acc* + *gen*	I am sorry for (*lit.*it makes X sorry for Y, *impers.*)
miseria -ae, f	sorrow, ordeal
misericordia -ae, f	pity
mitto, mittere, misi, missum	I send, throw, let go
modo	just now, only; (+ *subj*) provided that
modus -i, m	manner, way, kind
molior, moliri, molitus sum	I work at, attempt, strive to achieve
monumentum -i, n	monument, memorial
morbus -i, m	sickness, disease
morior, mori, mortuus sum	I die
mors, mortis, f	death
mortalis -e	mortal
muliebris -e	of a woman
multitudo, multitudinis, f	crowd, multitude
multus -a -um	much, many
municipium -i, n	town
munus, muneris, n	service, duty, present; public show
nato, natare, natavi, natatum	I swim, float, overflow
naufragium -i, n	shipwreck
nauseo, nauseare, nauseavi	I vomit
-ne	(introduces question)
ne ... quidem	not ... even
ne + *subj*	lest, (so) that not
nec, neque	and not, nor, neither
necesse (*indec*)	necessary
neco, necare, necavi, necatum	I kill

Vocabulary

nego, negare, negavi, negatum	I say no, deny, refuse, say that . . . not
negotium -i, n	business
nemo, nullius	no one, nobody
nepos, nepotis, m *and* **f**	grandchild
nequam (*indec. adj.*)	worthless, villainous
neque	*see* nec
nequitia -ae, f	worthlessness
nescio quis, nescio quid	some or other
nescio, nescire, nesci(v)i, nescitum	I do not know
nihil	nothing
nimirum	without doubt
nimis, nimium	too
nisi	unless, if not, except
nobilis -e	noble, famous
nolo, nolle, nolui + *infinitve*	I do not want, am unwilling, refuse to
nomen, nominis, n	name
non	not
non iam	no longer
nondum	not yet
nos, nostrum/nostri	we, us
noster, nostra, nostrum	our
notus -a -um	known, well-known, famous
novus -a -um	new, fresh, recent
nox, noctis, f	night
nudus -a -um	naked
nullus, nulla, nullum	no, none, not any
num	surely. . .not, whether
numerus -i, n	number
numquam	never

nunc	now
nundinae, nundinarum, f pl	(nine-day, weekly) market
nundinatio, nundinationis, f	trafficking
nuntiatio, nuntiationis, f	announcement
nuntio, nuntiare, nuntiavi, nuntiatum	I announce, report
obduresco, obdurescere, obdurui	I harden, become impervious to
obligo, obligare, obligavi, obligatum	I bind, oblige
obnuntio, obnuntiare, obnuntiavi, obnuntiatum + *dat*	I announce an omen unfavourable to
observo, observare, observavi, observatum	I pay heed to, respect
obses, obsidis, m *and* f	hostage
obsideo, obsidere, obsedi, obsessum	I besiege, blockade
obsolefio, obsolefieri, obsolefactus sum	I am degraded
obstringo, obstringere, obstrinxi, obstrictum	I hamper; oblige
obtineo, obtinere, obtinui, obtentum	I obtain; keep, preserve, observe
obvenio, obvenire, obveni, obventum	I fall to lot of; happen
obviam eo, ire, i(v)i + *dat*	I meet, go to meet, oppose, resist
occasio, occasionis, f	opportunity, occasion
occido, occidere, occidi, occisum	I kill
oculus -i, m	eye

odi, odisse (*perfect with present meaning*)	I hate
odium -i, n	hatred
offero, offerre, obtuli, oblatum	I present, offer
officium -i, n	duty, task, function
omitto, omittere, omisi, omissum	I neglect, disregard, make no mention of
omnino	altogether, at all, entirely
omnis -e	all, every
operio, operire, operui, opertum	I cover
opinor, opinari, opinatus sum	I suppose
oportet, oportere, oportuit	it is necessary, X ought, X must
oppidum -i, n	town
optimus -a -um	very good, best
opto, optare, optavi, optatum	I choose
opus, operis, n	work, toil, construction
oratio, orationis, f	speech
ordior, ordiri, orsus sum	I begin
ordo, ordinis, m	rank, order, line
orior, oriri, ortus sum	I rise, start, originate
oro, orare, oravi, oratum	I beg
os, oris, n	mouth, face
ostendo, ostendere, ostendi, ostentum	I show, point out, indicate
otium -i, n	leisure, idleness, peace
paene	almost, nearly
palleo, pallere, pallui	I grow pale
parens, parentis, m/f	parent; (pl) relations
pareo, parere, parui + *dat*	I obey

paries, parietis, m	wall
pario, parere, peperi, partum	I bear (a child), win, acquire, gain, secure
paro, parare, paravi, paratum	I prepare, provide
pars, partis, f	part, some, direction
partim	partly
parturio, parturire, parturi(v)i, parturitum	I am about to give birth to
parumper	for a little while
parvus -a -um	small
pateo, patere	I stand open
pater, patris, m	father
patientia -ae, f	passivity, acceptance
patior, pati, passus sum	I suffer, endur; (+ *inf*) allow
patres conscripti, m pl	senators
patrimonium -i, n	property, assets
patrius -a -um	of a father
patronus -i, m	patron
pauci -ae -a	few, a few
pavimentum -i, n	floor
pax, pacis, f	peace
pectus, pectoris, n	breast
pensio, pensionis, f	payment
per + *acc*	through, throughout, along
peragro, peragrare, peragravi, peragratum	I wander through, traverse
perbacchor, perbacchari, perbacchatus sum	I carouse unstoppably
percursatio, percursationis, f	romp, dash
perditus -a -um	dissolute
perdo, perdere, perdidi, perditum	I destroy, lose

peregrinatio, peregrinationis, f	wandering
pereo, perire, perii	I die, perish, am ruined
perfidia -ae, f	treachery
perfugium -i, n + *gen*	refuge from
perfungor, perfungi, perfunctus sum + *abl*	I discharge fully, carry out completely
periculum -i, n	danger
perpetuus -a – um	permanent
persequor, persequi, persecutus sum	I hound, pursue
persevero, perseverare, perseveravi, perseveratum	I persist
persono, personare, personui, personitum	I resound
perstringo, perstringere, perstrinxi, perstrictum	I graze lightly; narrate briefly
persuadeo, persuadere, persuasi, persuasum + *dat*	I persuade, convince
perterritus -a -um	very frightened, terrified
pertimesco, pertimescere, pertimui	I am very afraid of
perturbatio, perturbationis, f	disturbance
perturbo, perturbare, purturbavi, perturbatum	I disturb
pes, pedis, m	foot
pedem/me refero	retreat
petitio, petitionis, f	candidacy
peto, petere, petivi, petitum	I seek, ask for, make for, attack
pietas, pietatis, f	respect, dutiful conduct
placet, placere, placuit + *dat*	it pleases, suits, it is resolved
plangor, plangoris, m	lament, wailing
planus -a -um	obvious, plain

plausus, plausus, m	applause
plebs, plebis, f	the people, common people
plenus -a -um + *gen/abl*	full of, filled with
plurimus -a -um	very much, most
plus, pluris	more
poculum -i, n	cup, goblet
pono, ponere, posui, positum	I put, place, set up (camp)
populus -i, m	people, nation
porta -ae, f	gate
porticus, porticus, f	portico
porto, portare, portavi, portatum	I carry, bear, take
possessio, possessionis, f	possession
possum, posse, potui + *inf*	I can, am able to
post	afterwards, next
post + *acc*	behind, after
postea	afterwards, then
posterus -a -um	next
posthac	after this
postremus -a -um	last, ultimate
postulo, postulare, postulavi, postulatum	I demand, ask
potens	powerful
potestas, potestatis, f	power, authority, opportunity
potius	rather, more
praeclarus -a -um	splendid; famous
praeco, praeconis, m	herald; auctioneer
praedico, praedicare, preadicavi, praedicatum	I proclaim
praedico, praedicere, praedixi, praedictum	I foretell
praeditus -a -um + *abl*	endowed with

praedium -i, n	farm
praemium -i, n	prize, reward
praerogativus -a -um	first to be consulted, first to vote
praesertim	especially
praesidium -i, n	protection, garrison, fortification
praesum, praeesse, praefui + *dat*	I am in charge of
praeter + *acc*	beyond, except, besides
praeterea	besides, moreover, in addition
praeteritus -a -um	past
praetextatus -a -um	wearing the toga praetexta (see notes to 44 and 110)
praeverto, praevertere, praeverti + *acc* + *dat*	I attend to X before Y
prandium -i, n	lunch
primo	at first
primum	first of all
primus -a -um	first, chief
princeps, principis, m	emperor, chief, chieftain
principium -i, n	beginning
prius	before, previously
priusquam	before, until
privatus -a -um	private
pro + *abl*	in front of, for, on behalf of, in return for
probo, probare, probavi, probatum	I approve
procedo, procedere, processi, processum	I advance, proceed
procurator, procuratoris, m	agent

profero, proferre, protuli, prolatum	I bring forth, make public
proficiscor, proficisci, profectus sum	I set out, depart
profiteor, profiteri, professus sum	I make a declaration
prohibeo, prohibere, prohibui, prohibitum	I forbid; (+ *acc* + *abl*) debar from
promitto, promittere, promisi, promissum	I promise
promulgatio, promulgationis, f	accouncement, proclamation
promulgo, promulgare, promulgavi, promulgatum	I proclaim, announce
prope + *acc*	near
propter + *acc*	on account of, because of
prorogo, prorogare, prorogavi, prorogatum	I extend
prosterno, prosternere, prostravi, prostratum	I prostrate, throw oneself down
provideo, providere, providi, provisum	I foresee
provincia -ae, f	province
provoco, provocare, provocavi, provocatum	I challenge, provoke
proximus -a -um	nearest, next, last
prudentia -ae, f	intelligence
publicus -a -um	public, common
pudens, pudentis	decent, upright
puer, pueri, m	boy
pulcher, pulchra, pulchrum	beautiful
pulvinar, pulvinaris, n	couch (dedicated to god)
punctum -i, n	point

Vocabulary

purpureus -a -um	purple
Puteolanus -a -um	of Puteoli
puto, putare, putavi, putatum	I think, consider, reckon
quadratus -a -um	square
quaero, quaerere, quaesivi, quaesitum	I search for, ask for, ask, inquire
quaeso	(= *old form of* quaero) I beg, pray
quaestor, quaestoris, m	quaestor
quaestura -ae, f	quaestorship
quaestus, quaestus, m	gain, occupation
qualis -e	what sort of?
quam	how, than, as; what!
quam + *superlative*	as ... as possible
quamquam	although
quamvis + *subj*	although
quantus -a -um	how big; how much (*question or exclamation*)
quartus -a -um	fourth
quasi	as if, just as, nearly
quattuordecim	fourteen
-que	and
quem ad modum?	how?
queror, queri, questus sum	I complain
qui, quae, quod	who, which, that; (*interrog* which?)
quia	because
quibuscum	with whom (pl)
quicum, quocum	with whom (sing)
quid?	why?
quidam, quaedam, quoddam (*subst* **quiddam**)	one, a certain, some
quidem	indeed, in fact, however

quiesco, quiescere, quievi, quietum	I keep quiet
quilibet, quaelibet, quodlibet (*subst* **quidlibet**)	any; anyone, anything
quin etiam	yes, and ...
quintus -a -um	fifth
Quirinus -i, m	Quirinus, deified Romulus
quis?, quid?	who? what? anybody (after *si, ne, nisi, num*)
quisquam quicquam	anyone, anything
quisque, quaeque, quidque	each, each one, every
quisquis, quicquid	whoever, whatever
quivis, quaevis, quodvis (*subst* **quidvis**)	any whatever
quo	where to?; (*rel*) to where
quo modo?	how? in what way?
quoad	as long as, until
quod	because, (as to) the fact that
quod si	but if
quondam	once
quoniam	since
quotiens?	how often? as often as
rapina -ae, f	looting
ratio, rationis, f	account, reckoning; manner, means; reason
recipio, recipere, recepi, receptum	I regain, receive, accept, welcome
me recipio	I retreat, withdraw
recordatio, recordationis, f	remembrance
recordor, recordari, recordatus sum	I recall
rectus -a -um	straight, direct, right, proper

recupero, recuperare, recuperavi, recuperatum	I recover
reddo, reddere, reddidi, redditum	I give back, restore, hand over, make
redeo, redire, redii, reditum	I return, go back, come back
redimo, redimere, redemi, redemptum	I buy back, redeem
reditus, reditus, m	return
refero, referre, rettuli, relatum	I bring back, report, refer
regius – a -um	of a king
regno, regnare, regnavi, regnatum	I rule, govern
regnum -i, n	kingdom, reign, rule
reicio, reicere, reieci, reiectum	I reject
religio, religionis, f	reverence for gods, religious scruple
relinquo, relinquere, reliqui, relictum	I leave, leave behind, abandon
reliquus -a -um	the rest of, the other; subsequent
removeo, removere, removi, remotum	I remove
renuntio, renuntiare, renuntiavi, renuntiatum	I announce (officially)
repello, repellere, reppuli, repulsum	I repulse
repente	suddenly
reperio, reperire, repperi, repertum	I find
repraesento, repraesentare, repraesentavi, repraesentatum	I make present, actual again

requiro, requirere, requi(si)vi, requisitum	I inquire after
res publica, rei publicae, f	state, republic
res, rei, f	thing, affair, matter, business, property
resaluto, resalutare, resalutavi, resalutatum	I greet in reply
rescindo, rescindere, rescidi, rescissum	I rescind, repeal, abrogate
rescribo, rescribere, rescripsi, rescriptum	I write in reply, give as an expert opinion
respicio, respicere, respexi, respectum	I consider
respondeo, respondere, respondi, responsum	I answer, reply
revoco, revocare, revocavi, revocatum	I recall
rex, regis, m	king
rhetor, rhetoris, m	orator, teacher of rhetoric
rogo, rogare, rogavi, rogatum	I ask, ask for
Romanus -a -um	Roman
rostra -orum, n pl	rostra, speakers' platform
rursus	back, again; on the other hand
sacerdos, sacerdotis, m and f	priest, priestess
sacerdotium -i, n	priestly office
saeculum -i, n	century, age
saepio, saepire, saepsi, saeptum	I fence in
sagitta -ae, f	arrow
salus, salutis, f	health, safety, greeting
salutaris -e	beneficial, healthy
saluto, salutare, salutavi, salutatum	I greet, salute

salvus -a -um	healthy, sound, safe
sanctus -a -um	holy
sane	indeed, for certain
sano, sanare, sanavi, sanatum	I cure
sanus -a -um	sane
sapientia -ae, f	wisdom, good sense
satelles, satellitis, m/f	member of retinue
satis	enough
satisfacio, satisfacere, satisfeci, satisfactum + *dat*	I give satisfaction to
sceleratus -a -um	wicked
scelus, sceleris, n	crime, wickedness
scio, scire, scivi, scitum	I know
scortum -i, n	prostitute
scutum -i, n	shield
se, sui	himself, herself, itself, themselves
secundus -a -um	following, next, second; favourable
sed	but
sedeo, sedere, sedi, sessum	I sit
sedo, sedare, sedavi, sedatum	I allay, settle
sella -ae, f	seat
semper	always
semustilatus -a -um	half-burned
senatus, senatus, m	senate
senex, senis, m	old man
sensus, sensus, m	sense, sensibility
sententia -ae, f	opinion, judgement, sentence
sentio, sentire, sensi, sensum	I feel, notice, hear, judge
sequor, sequi, secutus sum	I follow, pursue, attend
serus -a -um	late
servio, servire, servi(v)I, servitum	I am a slave

servitus, servitutis, f	slavery
servo, servare, servavi, servatum	I save, protect, keep; observe, watch for
servus -i, m	slave
sestertius -i, m	sestertius
sexagie(n)s	sixty times
si	if
si minus	if not
sic	thus, in this way
Sidicini, Sidicinorum, m pl	Sidicini, a people of Campania
signum -i, n	sign, signal, standard; statue
similis -e + *gen or dat*	similar to, like
simplex, simplicis	simple
simul	at the same time, together
simulac, simulatque	as soon as
simulacrum -i, n	image
sin	if, however
sine + *abl*	without
singillatim	one by one
singularis -e	peculiar
singulus -a -um	individual
sive, seu	or if, whether
sobrius -a -um	sober
societas, societatis, f	alliance
socius -i, m (*also* **-a, -um)**	ally, comrade, companion, business partner
soleo, solere, solitus sum	I am accustomed
solum	only
solus -a -um	alone, only, lonely, single
sors, sortis, f	luck, lot
sortitio, sortitionis, f	choice by lot
species, speciei, f	semblance, outward form

spectio, spectionis, f	watching, taking (of omens)
spero, sperare, speravi, speratum	I hope, expect
spes, spei, f	hope
sponte (+ gen/possess)	on the initiative of
stabilis -e	stable
statim	at once, immediately
stimulus -i, m	goad
stipo, stipare, stipavi, stipatum	I pack densely, surround closely
sto, stare, steti, statum	I stand, stand firm
stola -ae, f	dress, robe, gown
strenuus -a -um	energetic
studium -i, n	eagerness, study, devotion
stultus -a -um	stupid, foolish
stupiditas, stupiditatis, f	stupidity
stupor, stuporis, m	numbness
stuprum -I, n	sexual misdemeanour, disgrace
suavitas, suavitatis, f	pleasantness
subito	suddenly
sudo, sudare, sudavi, sudatum	I sweat
suffragium -i, n	vote; cavalry voting group
sum, esse, fui	I am
summus -a -um	highest, greatest, top (of)
sumo, sumere, sumpsi, sumptum	I take, take up
supplex, supplicis, m	suppliant
supplicatio, supplicationis, f	thanksgiving
supplicium -i, n	punishment
suspicio, suspicionis, f	suspicion
suus -a -um	his (own), her (own), its (own), their (own)
tabula -ae, f	tablet, notice, list; picture

taceo, tacere, tacui, tacitum	I am quiet
talis -e	such
tam	so
tamen	however, nevertheless, yet
tamquam	as if, as though
tandem	at last, finally; (in questions) I ask you
tantum	only
tantus -a -um	so great, such a great, so much
tarditas, tarditatis, f	sluggishness
tectum -i, n	roof, house
tegula -ae, f	roof tile
Tellus, Telluris, f	Earth
temeritas, temeritatis, f	rashness, heedlessness
templum -i, n	temple
tempto, temptare, temptavi, temptatum	I make trial of, test
tempus, temporis, n	time
teneo, tenere, tenui, tentum	I hold, keep, maintain
terra -ae, f	ground, land, earth
territorium -i, n	territory
tertius -a -um	third
testamentum -i, n	will
timeo, timere, timui	I fear, am afraid
timor, timoris, m	fear, anxiety
toga -ae, f	toga
tollo, tollere, sustuli, sublatum	I raise, lift up, remove, destroy
totus -a -um	the whole, entire, all
tranquillus -a -um	peaceful
transfero, transferre, transtuli, translatum/tralatum	I transfer, switch

Vocabulary

transilio, transilire, transili(v)i	I leap across, skip over
tres, tria	three
tribunatus, tribunatus, m	tribunate
tribuo, tribuere, tribui, tributum	I grant
tu, tui	you (singular)
tum	then, next
turbo, turbare, turbavi, turbatum	I upset
turpis -e	shameful
turpitudo, turpitudinis, f	disgrace
tuus, tua, tuum	your (singular)
tyrannus -i, m	tyrant
ubi	where? where, when
ubicumque	wherever
ulciscor, ulcisci, ultus sum	I avenge
ullus, ulla, ullum	any
ultimus -a -um	furthest, last, utmost
ultro	of own accord
umquam	ever
una	together
unde	from where, whence
universus -a -um	whole
unus -a -um	one, alone
urbs, urbis, f	city, town, Rome
usquam	anywhere
usque	all the way, right up to, continuously
usque quaque	in every respect
ut + *indic*	as, where, when, how
ut + *subj*	that, so that, to
uterque, utraque, utrumque	each (of two), both

utinam (+ *subj*)	would that . . .!
utor, uti, usus sum + *abl*	I use, enjoy
valeo, valere, valui	I am strong, have influence, am valid
valva -ae, f	(folding) door
-ve	or
vectigal, vectigalis, n	tax, government revenue
vel	or, either
venditio, venditionis, f	sale
vendo, vendere, vendidi, venditum	I sell
veneo, venire, veni(v)i, venitum	I am sold
veneror, venerari, veneratus sum	I revere
venio, venire, veni, ventum	I come
verbum -i, n	word
verecundus -a -um	modest, decent
vereor, vereri, veritus sum	I fear, am afraid
vero	indeed, in fact, however
versor, versari, versatus sum	I remain, dwell
verum	but, however
verus -a -um	true, real
veteranus -i, m	veteran
vexillum -i n	standard
vexo, vexare, vexavi, vexatum	I provoke, annoy
via -ae, f	street, road, way, path
vicinus -i, m	neighbour
video, videre, vidi, visum	I see
videor, videri, visus sum	I seem, appear, am seen
viginti	twenty
villa -ae, f	country-house, estate, farm
vinolentia -ae, f	wine-bibbing, drunken orgy

vinum -i, n	wine
vir, viri, m	man, husband
virilis -e	of a man
vis, pl vires, f	force, violence; (pl) strength, forces
vita -ae, f	life
vitio, vitiare, vitiavi, vitiatum	I declare void
vitiosus -a -um	flawed; elected under an unfavourable sign
vitium -i, n	fault; unfavourable sign
vivo, vivere, vixi	I live, am alive, (+ abl) live on
vivus -a- um	alive, living
vix	hardly, scarcely, with difficulty
voco, vocare, vocavi, vocatum	I call, summon, invite, name
volgaris -e (= vulgaris)	common-or-garden, ordinary
volo, velle, volui + *infinitive*	I want, wish, am willing, intend
voluntas, voluntatis, f	wish
vomer, vomeris, m	ploughshare
vomo, vomere, vomui, vomitum	I spew up
vos, vestrum/vestri	you (plural)
vox, vocis, f	voice, shout, word
vulnus, vulneris, n	wound, injury